RALPH WALDO EMERSON
An Interpretive Essay

RALPH WALDO EMERSON

An Interpretive Essay

BY

LEWIS LEARY

BOSTON

TWAYNE PUBLISHERS

RALPH WALDO EMERSON

Copyright © 1980 by Lewis Leary
All Rights Reserved

Published by Twayne Publishers
A Division of G. K. Hall & Co.
70 Lincoln Street, Boston, Massachusetts 02111

Designed by Thomas T. Beeler

Printed on permanent/durable acid-free paper and bound
in the United States of America

First Printing

Library of Congress Cataloging in Publication Data

Leary, Lewis Gaston, 1906–
Ralph Waldo Emerson : an interpretive essay.

(Twayne's related titles)
Bibliography: p. 169–70
1. Emerson, Ralph Waldo, 1803–1882—Criticism
and interpretation.
PS1638.L4   814′.3   79–25860
ISBN 0–8057–9012–8

For Margaret and David Brunn
First Readers

The idea of unconditioned spirit is of course a very old one, but we are probably the first people to think of it as a realistic possibility and to make that possibility a part of our secret assumption.

—Lionel Trilling, *The Opposing Self*

Preface

THIS BOOK had its origin many years ago in a series of talks to an adult audience interested in continuing education. All or some parts of it have been repeated and expanded as lectures or in seminar conversations at the University of North Carolina, Columbia University, Johns Hopkins University, the University of Pennsylvania, Swarthmore College, and the University of Texas, and abroad at the American Seminar at Rome, the University of Amsterdam, the University of Munich, the University of Teheran, the University of Jordan, and Guanabara University in Brazil.

It is not intended for those who know Emerson well and recognize his radical simplicity and soaring multiplicity. It is rather meant for those who have been introduced to Emerson only in part, to whom he has perhaps been presented as a simple man of impracticable idealism, inappropriate to our less optimistic generation.

If the reader finds this book repetitious, it is because Emerson was unshamedly repetitious, circling about a few radical ideas that have seemed to me to have become what Lionel Trilling has called "part of our secret assumption."

In its preparation I have been indebted to many people whose ideas and explanations have been assimilated into my own. Chief among them are the late Stephen Whicher, who suggested that I make this attempt, and the late Ralph Leslie Rusk, who saw portions of it as it began but might not approve of the large steps I have taken to make it plain. Others will hear echoes of their voices, rephrased to my idiom: to all of them, great thanks. Students over many years have been especially helpful, constructively critical: chief among them have been John Auchard, Thomas Beeler, William Craft, Ronald Hoag, Carla Mazzini, Richard Robey, and Dorothy Scura, seminarians who dared talk back to

Ralph Waldo Emerson

their professor. David and Margaret Brunn, Lewis and Frances Gray Patton, Louis D. Rubin, Jr., and, again, John Auchard provided patient and pertinent final commentary.

LEWIS LEARY

Chapel Hill, 1979

Contents

Illustrations

The Responsibility of Man

I

The Quest for Vocation

R ALPH WALDO EMERSON was perhaps the most influential American of his generation. He inspired thousands and he angered thousands because he incited people
to think, and on levels beyond those to which they were
accustomed. His genius and his continuing accomplishment
was that he could startle people, not necessarily into agree-
ment with what he said, but into the sometimes unusual
but always satisfying experience of having a thought which
was or seemed to be their own. Most of them knew, however, that to resist Emerson was ultimately as important
as to accept him. He urges each reader to think his own
thoughts, stand on his own feet, act in his own manner.
Reading him with care inevitably results in recognition of
the paradox that one may be Emersonian and yet agree with
scarcely a word that Emerson says.

Underlying everything that he does say is one simple
question. What, he asks, is a person to do with a life so
mysteriously bestowed, so like and yet so different from that
of anyone else? "What," he would ask himself, "is to be
the substance of my shrift?" What am I, a single, separate
person, to do that I may identify myself, be what I am
able to be, thus to repay my debt to nature of which I am
a part, but from which, being my own self, I may stand
apart, defying or submitting to its inexorable requirements?

He asks the question of himself and, after years of quest-
ing, comes up with this answer: that each person is to live
to fullest capacity in accordance with whatever gifts have
been supplied or denied, neither striving for the accom-

plishment of more than can be accomplished, nor settling for the accomplishment of less. No sin is greater than dissipation, no virtue larger than concentration. Emerson invites to introspection. He demands self-confidence. "Trust thy self: every heart," he says, "vibrates to that iron string. Accept the place divine providence has found for you. . . . Insist on yourself; never imitate. . . . Nothing can bring you peace but yourself."

Such buoyant confidence may now seem old-fashioned, reminders of older, less cluttered and complicated times. Some will dismiss Emerson, as T. S. Eliot did, as a man who has outlived his influence, to become an encumbrance, even an embarrassment. Positivists will find him slippery—a man, it has been said, without a handle, without intellectual precision or philosophical consistency. Others, confirmed in conviction that their world is roiled by evil and stained by sin, will shrug away from Emerson because he seems to say that there is no such thing as evil, that evil is only the absence of good—which indeed it may be. Many will chuckle over what Sidney Lanier said of Emerson: "He took me by the hand and led me nowhere, and said many wise and beautiful things along the way." They may agree with H. L. Mencken that he is a "moon-struck parson," whose sugary and soaring optimism "sets up a magnificent glow without adding any destructive heat."

Everyone, it may be said, gets the Emerson he deserves. Read in part, he is understood in part. Fragmented, he can provide arguments that seem to lead in diverse directions. Read whole, he is, as Erwin Edman once explained, "all of a piece, and to turn to him at some late, quiet hours of the night is to come inevitably, familiarly, and with quickening excitement upon his familiar theme or, more accurately, his variations on a theme." He may be, as Hyatt Waggoner has suggested, the font from which subsequent American writing, specifically its poetry, has received richest sustenance. Or he may be the man who Quentin Anderson has testified attempted to lift himself by his own bootstraps, leaving a legacy of consuming introspective self-interest which has tainted our literature, depriving it of a rightful heritage of recognized tradition. Whatever he was, Emerson was consistently there, daring to flaunt inevitable inconsistencies, continually a challenge, inviting response. His voice continues to beguile, inspire, or antagonize. "No one," Henry Seidel Canby has testified, "can possibly understand his country, either what it was, what it has become, or what it may be, or comprehend its unexpected moral strength or its (to Americans) equally unexpected moral weaknesses, unless he knows his Emerson."

Surely, he was the supreme egotist, certain in every certainty. His entire thought in paradigm is cryptically encompassed in three words from his early essay on *Nature:* "I see all," or even more enigmatically in the familiar play on what James Russell Lowell called the first-person perpendicular, "I, eye, aye." The individual, the "I," is supreme; his perception, his "eye," is his entry to reality; through his perception he may discover and without hesitation apprehend and without questioning accept all things with a confident "aye," sure in knowledge that each is contained in all.

But his perception is not only physical. There was for him a means of apprehending reality that transcends the senses: that is what makes Emerson a Transcendentalist. Apprehension may come from within, a current of universal being, so that man becomes a "part or parcel of God." Therefore, he counseled his countrymen, "believe that what is true for you in your own heart is true for all men." It was not in diffidence that he proclaimed, "I am nothing; I see all." He knew that he could with confidence lose himself in the immensity of all being.

Through all that Emerson wrote, ran this single theme, on which he played a multitude of variations. His first collection of *Essays* began, "There is one mind common to all individual men." Man, he said, is the measure and measurer of all things. Man must survey the world, for he alone can identify it for what it is. He must see it as it is today, as if he were the first man, seeing it for the first time. "Our age," he scolded, "is retrospective." It looks backwards. It feeds on the past. It accepts creeds which are outworn. It gives unthinking lip-service to notions which have no present effective validity: "It builds the sepulchres of the fathers. It writes biographies, histories and criticism." Though "foregoing generations beheld God and nature face to face," we behold them only "through their eyes."

Emerson was in every sense revolutionary. He called on his countrymen to advance by thinking for themselves, not simply to tread without thought in the footsteps of others. He challenged them to fumble no longer among the dead bones of the past, but to build their own systems, create their own patterns of living, each person according to his or her own ability. Creeds—whether Anglican, Unitarian, or Presbyterian, Republican or Democrat—were for slothful men, for men willing to accept without thinking the opinion of those who went before them. "If a man is wise," said Emerson, "he will say to himself, I am not a member of that or of any party. I am God's child, a disciple of Christ, or in the eye of God, a fellow disciple with Christ. . . . A sect or party is an elegant incognito devised to save men from thinking." And around this theme he constantly revolves, circling back to it again and again, in manifold variations.

What then is a man to do with his life, if he is to live it satisfactorily, honestly, perceptively? What is the measure of human greatness? Emerson did not come easily to the answer to his question. His own quest for vocation was not without troublesome hesitations. He was a long time discovering the part which he should play in life, which could bring the peace within himself for which he relentlessly sought. Born in Boston in 1803, into a provincial culture which was not to come of age for several decades (and then in large part through Emerson's influence), he was the oldest of the writers who, as the century moved on, were

The Quest for Vocation

responsible for what has been called the flowering of New England. He was four years old when Longfellow and Whittier were born. He was the pious six-year-old son of a popular Boston clergyman when in that city a pair of strolling players produced their second son, and called him Edgar Poe. And in that same year his father's clerical friend, the Rev. Asher Holmes, had a son whom he called Oliver Wendell after his wife's wealthy, merchant relatives. Melville, Thoreau, Whitman, and Lowell—each of whom was to grow under or away from the influence of Emerson—were born while he was an undergraduate at Harvard, discovering Wordsworth, reading first in Coleridge.

We need to place Emerson thus against his contemporaries, and we need also to see him in relation to his own past. "Every book," he said, "is a quotation, and every house is a quotation out of all forests and mines and stone quarries; and every man is a quotation from all his ancestors." So we do not understand Emerson unless we know something of the stock from which he sprang. No family in all New England better illustrated Oliver Wendell Holmes's description of a Brahmin caste. Behind Emerson were eight generations of clergymen, cultured, conscientious, and practical. His grandfather had been the first occupant of the Old Manse at Concord and had preached a sermon on the Sunday before the battle of Concord bridge on the theme of "Resistance to Tyrants Is Obedience to God." These clergymen ancestors were men to be proud of—they had been leaders of men, solid in thought, firm in conviction. The memory of their accomplishment haunted young Emerson. "From childhood," he confided to his diary, "the names of the great have ever resounded in my ear, and it is impossible that I should be indifferent to the rank which I must take in the innumerable assembly of men."

Emerson's father himself set a pattern of excellence. He was a fashionable, successful clergyman in Boston, a man of social habits, of literary taste, chaplain of the State Senate, a founder of learned societies, one of the editors of the

Ralph Waldo Emerson

literary *Monthly Anthology*. William Emerson was an outgoing, handsome gentleman, tall and of confidently commanding presence; he was welcome at dinners, literary conversations, and civic occasions. But his career was cut short in 1811 when at forty-two he died of tuberculosis. His loss was felt throughout the city, but most poignantly by his widow, left with little money and with five young sons to educate.

Someone will someday tell the fascinating story of the Emersons of this generation, of the five brothers left fatherless, of the heroic sacrifices of the mother, of the drill-sergeant instruction of Mary Moody Emerson, their maiden aunt, their dead father's sister, a peppery gentlewoman, little more than four feet tall and dedicated to the proposition that all Emersons had inborn responsibility to become famous men. In 1811, when their father died, William, the oldest son, was ten; Ralph Waldo was eight; Edward, six; Bulkeley, five; and Charles, three. It soon became evident that Bulkeley was never going to develop mentally; but the progress of the other brothers, through the Boston Latin School, and then to Harvard, one after another, the older helping the younger by teaching school during vacations, by organizing schools of their own after graduation; and the younger in their turn teaching school so that the older now might go on with graduate work—this saga of family cooperation and aspiration, through poverty and ill health, has never been completely told.

For years the family lived a spartan existence, practicing necessary economies, learning to be frugal, to make the most of what they had—like one overcoat for two boys, worn alternately. The poverty of the Emerson family after 1811 was the harder to bear because it was a genteel poverty. Appearances had to be maintained, family pride bolstered. The boys were read stories of spartan courage by their dedicated aunt. Their mother reminded them that as Emersons they were expected to be successful. Poverty of this

The Quest for Vocation

kind can stiffen a boy's spine, but it can also cramp and cripple him: it can lead a proud young man to vow that never, if he can possibly avoid it, will he be poor again. The worst of poverty was that one was beholden, dependent. Something of individuality is lost, something of self-assurance. Pride is bruised, but made stronger also. These spare years affected Emerson in each of these ways. They stiffened him to stubborn resolution, but they also left him pinched and niggardly so that for the rest of his life he hoarded worldly things as he hoarded thoughts, as if he feared material as well as intellectual poverty. He called his journal his savings bank and, miserlike, crammed it full of his and other men's thoughts, from which he drew dividends in lectures, essays, and poems.

An examination of the personalities and characters of the brothers and of Emerson's place among them will explain something of this wariness, this carefulness, this kind of personal conservatism which was always to characterize him. William, the oldest brother, was hard-working and dependable; he did well at Harvard and then established a successful girls' school in Boston. When it came his time for graduate study, he went abroad to read theology in Germany, but something of the doubting spirit of the time troubled him, so that he left the ministry to study law in New York—this after an interview with Goethe at Weimar, in which the German poet recommended to him the kind of expediency which was to be useful also in determining the career of William's next younger brother. "The highest aim in life," Goethe had told him, "should be for each one to accommodate himself as perfectly as possible to the state in which he was placed." There was something just deterministic enough about this to appeal to young men brought up in but rebelling against a Calvinist background: the advice suggested predestination, that one must do what was fated for him to do; but it spoke also of freedom from the

9

necessity of doing what custom decreed—like becoming a minister or remaining a New Englander simply because one's father had been one.

If William was the steady and conscientious brother, who was to become a judge in New York and have a hill on Staten Island named for him, Edward and Charles were the brilliant ones, and Waldo was the least promising of the four—he was the frivolous one, less serious than the others. At college, although a scholarship student, he graduated among the bottom half of his class, and was chosen class poet only after six others had declined the honor. Waldo was literary rather than studious—he wrote plays and poems, and even short romances in prose. "I would plunge," he said, "into the classic lore of chivalrous story" in search of "splendid forms and gorgeous fancies." Such truant thoughts as these stretched his young imagination, but helped little with collegiate exercises.

His younger brother Edward, however, graduated triumphantly at the head of his class. Charles did almost as well a few years later, and with the added reputation of being a brilliant orator, universally admired. As he watched his gifted younger brothers, Emerson worried about himself: "I find myself often idle, vagrant, stupid, and hollow," he confessed. Among his Harvard classmates, he felt "a humiliating sense of inferiority." He confided to his journal, "All around me are industrious and will be great. I am indolent and will be insignificant!" And, he admonished, "if I do not discipline myself with diligent care, I shall suffer severely from remorse and the sense of inferiority thereafter." As he turned nineteen, he wondered, "Has any other educated person lived so many years and lost so many days?"

Yet it was to be precisely this lack of discipline that finally saved Emerson. Like Edward and Charles, he suffered greatly from ill health. Each of them was early threatened by tuberculosis; each took long trips to the South in search of relief. In Emerson the disease was finally arrested, but the two younger, more brilliant brothers died early, their physical disease aggravated, it has been suggested, by some obscure psychological weakening of the will to live.

Edward had struggled desperately to measure up to his own and his family's expectations, and he seemed to have succeeded. He was studying law under the sponsorship of New England's greatest man, Daniel Webster, when he broke down completely. "I tho't," he wrote from the deep of his despair, "to find [God] in the hurricane of ambition —but He was not there. . . . Faint and weary, I have fallen prostrate." Similarly Charles, the most well roundedly accomplished of the brothers, was also haunted by demons which threatened failure. Were all minds, he wondered, racked as his with doubt and self-accusation? Only Waldo, of whom less was expected, marshaled his forces, rested, allowed nature to take its course, and in time recovered, even improved in health. He learned early to recognize limitations. He was frugal. He measured himself against life and cautiously took from it only what was his.

But his conscience continued to plague him. "I must improve my time better," he reminded himself. "I must prepare myself for the great profession I have purposed to undertake." Alone among the brothers he was to follow the family vocation of clergyman. "I am to give my soul to God and withdraw from sin and the world the idle or vicious time and thoughts I have sacrificed to them." But this was never to be easy—perhaps because he was unable to accept the terms in which he had been taught to phrase it. The business of the church, he thought, was to encourage right living rather than reinforce religious dogma. Preaching he might manage, for that then in vogue seemed to him to depend "chiefly on imagination for its success" so that in spite of his "reasoning faculty" being "proportionately weak," he might do, and did do, well enough, though he continued to be beset by what he described as "my cardinal sin of dissipation—sinful strolling from book to book, from care to idleness."

11

Ralph Waldo Emerson

He was not consistently a student. He had no talent for the kind of logical discipline that theology or philosophy or even science required. He had no mind for the simpler logic of law. He blushed and stammered when he tried to teach. Yet he was physically and temperamentally unfit for anything but one of the professions—farming certainly would not do, nor the life of a merchant. It seemed to him as it does to many young men that he was born to be independent of such things as making a living. But he was not independent. What, therefore, was he to do with his life? Goethe had told his brother that no one was to do what he was not qualified to do. What was he qualified to do? For more than a dozen years after he left college in 1821 the answer to this question was to be Emerson's quest.

He lived most of these years in what Van Wyck Brooks has called a House of Pain. They were years of illness, frustration, false beginnings, calamity, and confusion. Threatened constantly with tuberculosis, he also suffered from eye failure and rheumatism. He could not even preach without pain from "the mouse" in his chest: "My lungs," he said, "sing sexton and sorrow whenever I ask them to shout a sermon for me." Then Edward went suddenly insane: "Edward, the admired, the learned, eloquent, striving boy, a maniac." Bulkeley became increasingly subject to fits of blind rage which made it necessary to send him away. "We are born to trouble," Emerson wrote his older brother William, and he worried about his own sanity. "When I consider," he said, "the constitutional calamity of my family, which, in its falling upon Edward, has buried at once so many towering hopes—with whatever reason, I have little apprehension of my own liability to the same evil. I have such a mixture of *silliness* in my intellectual frame that I think Providence has tempered me against this. My brother lived and acted and spoke with preternatural energy. My own manner is sluggish; my speech flippant, sometimes embarrassed and ragged; my actions (if I may say so) are of a passive kind. Edward always had great power of face. I have none. I laugh; I blush; I look ill-tempered, against my will and against my interest." But he was beginning to suspect now that these imperfections of his might be ballasts, defenses against excess, anchors to sanity. A man might make a virtue of his imperfections. For every weakness could there not be some compensating strength?

During the next few years Emerson sorely needed whatever ballast he could find. As a clergyman he did not do badly at first. When his chest held out, he preached well, with a certain cold intensity that passed for dignity. Before he had a regular charge of his own, he occupied the pulpit in one outlying church or another, cannily making one sermon stretch over several Sundays. He wrote sermons slowly, and he wrote them out in full, as he later would his lectures, for he never got over a hesitancy about extempore speaking in public. Then, in northern New Hampshire, where he served one congregation for several weeks, he met and fell in love with seventeen-year-old Ellen Tucker, the frail and talented daughter of a well-to-do family. Like him she was a poet, and she was so ill with tuberculosis that she made even a man with lungs as weak as Emerson's feel strong in the thought of protecting her. Their love was the sturdiest thing about this pair. It sustained each of them against the crippling onslaught of life. It was holy and invigorating. "A mind might ponder its thoughts for ages," Emerson later wrote, "and not gain so much self-knowledge as the passion of love shall teach it in a day."

They were married a year later, soon after he at twenty-six accepted a call to which, he said, "all the years of my education have looked forward." He was asked to be a minister at the Old Second Church in Boston, the same church in which the great Increase and Cotton Mather had formerly presided. The ugly duckling son had finally, un-

Ralph Waldo Emerson

believably, succeeded. It was fortune not beyond his dream, but beyond his expectation. He was settled into a living that could bring prestige. The Emerson family tradition would not be broken. For the first time in his memory he was independent, freed from poverty. He had a good salary, a good house to live in, and a wife who brought him not only great happiness, but additional income besides. He was elected chaplain of the Senate as his father had been; he was appointed to the school board; he was listened to with respect and affection.

But he continued to be troubled about how poorly qualified he was for the position he held. His studies had been mainly pursued in private, interrupted by ill-health and school teaching. He must have recognized his grasp of them as superficial—how poorly grounded he was in theology and metaphysics. His only real intellectual acquisition was literary, and that mostly in poetry rather than in reasoned prose. Religiously he was decadent, not only a protestant Unitarian, but responding dangerously to notions of Swedenborg and Coleridge rather than to the fathers of the church. "I hate steady labour from noon till night," he said, "and therefore am not a learned man, but I have an omnivorous curiosity." His belief was diluted with heresy.

When Ellen died eighteen months after their marriage, Emerson's happy new world fell in ruins around him. The grief in losing her seemed more than he could bear. He exhausted himself by walking miles each day to visit the cemetery where she lay. Months after her burial he begged that her grave be opened so that he might see her once more. Life was suddenly gray. The poetry was gone, together with the love and the liveliness. Suddenly he realized that he was not really doing well as a clergyman. He looked with dismay toward the endless succession of Sundays that stretched ahead of him, each with its demand for a fresh sermon. He was not prepared. He was not even sure what he believed. He rebelled against religious formalities, the empty repetitiousness of ritual. So he resigned his charge and quit

The Quest for Vocation

the ministry. "It is my desire," he told his congregation, "to do nothing which I cannot do with my whole heart."

More independent now because of a small legacy from his deceased wife's estate, but beset by sorrow and illness and increased uncertainty of what was his true vocation, he went abroad on a literary pilgrimage, during which he called on Landor, Coleridge, Wordsworth, and Carlyle. The world was blank and bleak and lonely, and he was unsure and ill at ease in the presence of these literary giants of an older generation. Disappointed in so many things, he was saddened to find himself disappointed in them also. They seemed to lack moral fiber or a high and dedicated seriousness. They were of another generation, and repetitious—all but Carlyle were voices from the past. None of them provided the relief that the grieving young widower so desperately required. If not the church, if not among the poets, where then would he find solace? Where direction? Or purpose? Emerson looked long and deeply into himself.

He returned to the United States, still discouraged but somewhat mended in mind and body. He did some lecturing and occasional preaching. He was increasingly drawn toward becoming a writer—but of what kind, to what purpose, what effect? How was he to conduct his life now that he was free to live it as he wished, freed from the ugly impediment of poverty? He took heart as he planned things that he and his brothers might do together. They might keep a school. They might manage a magazine. But then Edward died, and then Charles, and Emerson was left alone—defeated, he must have felt, at every turn.

He would marry again four years after his first wife's death, and settle quietly into living at Concord. In the eyes of his family and of his neighbors he was a man of no occupation who spent his time to no apparent purpose over books. He had once thought he would be a poet, but much of poetry had been driven from him: he was poet, he thought, in everything but words, and that in the eyes of the world was no poet at all. He was clearly unsuccessful as a clergyman—though he supplied occasionally in other men's pulpits for several years. He had, as has been said, too inconsecutive a mind to be a philosopher or even a lawyer. He was shy, withdrawn, wounded, unsure. His father, his favorite and most promising brothers, and his beloved young wife had all died of the same dread disease that daily menaced him. He had seen how brilliant minds broke from overwork or overreaching. Never could the husbanding of what strength he had have seemed more important to him. What can a man do with his life when he is thus crippled?

The longer he pondered it, the clearer seemed the answer. A man might in truth make a virtue of his weaknesses. Each man must seek out carefully what he was best fitted to do. Any other path led inevitably to destruction. Was not this the burden of what Goethe had told his brother many years before? Was it not the moral behind Edward's collapse and Charles's death, and perhaps even Ellen's? Man at his own peril flies too close to the sun.

Mortal man must know boundaries beyond which he cannot travel, yet within those boundaries may discover a place uniquely his own. If he cannot think logically, then perhaps for him logical thinking is not important—perhaps it is really not important for anyone. If he cannot concentrate in his reading, but instead finds his mind rising responsive to a single thought and disregarding all the rest—then perhaps these single thoughts are important. If a man must live quietly to conserve his physical or even his mental health—then perhaps quiet living is the thing.

Emerson spent the rest of his life devising an attitude toward living that could be satisfying to a man crippled as he was. He outlines it in expansive detail, but not for our imitating: he suggests that all people seek an attitude of their own, cut to the measure of their own inevitable

The Quest for Vocation

shortcomings. He invites recognition that every person is somehow crippled, and no two in quite the same manner. Yet he would have them confident that each is capable of finding a way toward truth. It would not matter that our way was not his way. Each man, as Edwin Arlington Robinson, paraphrasing Emerson, put it, must find his way alone. No one else can find it for him. He must have the courage and the wisdom to trust himself.

Emerson put the whole of his philosophy in capsule form into a little book which he published in 1836, when he was thirty-three, and which sold very poorly. He called it *Nature*, and intended it as the first of a pair of books, the second of which (never written) was to be called *Spirit*. Everything he was ever to say was said in minuscule in *Nature*, but woven so tightly that readers have had difficulty in unraveling its strands of meaning. A year later with "The American Scholar," then the next year with "The Divinity School Address," and shortly thereafter in such essays as "Self-Reliance" and "Experience," he began to expand his ideas, spelling them out slowly and carefully, and his fame began to grow.

It was not until three years after his first book appeared that Emerson, at thirty-six, finally articulated his conception of what his role in life would be. "What," he asked himself then, "shall be the substance of my shrift?"—what is to be my place in the world, I who am neither preacher nor teacher nor philosopher, nor successfully what the world calls poet. He gives his answer with confidence now: "Adam in the garden, I am to new name all the beasts in the fields and all the gods in the sky. I am to invite men drenched in Time to recover themselves & come out of time, and taste their native immortal air. I am to fire with what skill I can the artillery of sympathy & emotion. I am to indicate constantly, though all unworthy, the Ideal and Holy Life, the life within life,—the Forgotten Good, the Unknown Cause in which we sprawl & sin. I am to try the magic of sincerity, that luxury permitted only to kings and poets.

Ralph Waldo Emerson

I am to celebrate the spiritual powers in their infinite contrast to the mechanical powers and the mechanical philosophy of this time. I am to console the brave sufferers under evils whose end they cannot see by appeals to the great optimism, self-affirmed in all bosoms."

In his country about him he saw men living lives unworthy of their manhood, so burdened with flesh that there was no room for spirit. In the midst of the new and brash and boastful and expanding American democracy of the 1830s, shot through with cant and hypocrisy, he would discover a democracy of spirit where people meet on equal terms. He would be Columbus to this new world, and he would discover it through seeing the world about him as it was. He would try the magic of sincerity in seeing the world fresh, not as tradition bade him see it. He would trust his own eyes, his own senses; he would see it as the first man saw it before he was beguiled by worldly things. He would see it as a child sees it, as a poet, or an innocent sees it—as if it has never been seen before.

To be sincere, to be simple, to be himself and not what others expected him to be—that, he thought, was enough. Sitting quietly in Concord he built a world upon these elementary notions. It is his world, and may or may not be ours. But we must know its geography if we are to comprehend the literature and the lives it has encouraged, and also those that have risen in questioning rebellion against it. That exploration can provide some pleasure, perhaps some exasperation, but finally some profit, if only in discovering traits of strangeness within ourselves and in the world which we inhabit and inevitably distort to fit our expectations. Emerson's requirements are not large, and they may not be precisely our own. Whether the fault is his or ours, each must in his own manner determine.

Emerson was to live long in Concord and raise a family there. He lectured widely, puttered in his garden, and wrote books. His life was outwardly calm, though not without occasional depths of sorrow. He led no crusades, and in his later years he became a frugal man of means. But his true life story is discovered not in the man of day-by-day activities, but in his transformation of thought to art, handed down as a legacy to all who, like him, would in their better moments find satisfaction in recognizing the supremacy of spirit.

II

The Infinitude of the Private Man

IT IS NOT, I think, reading too much into Emerson's life to discover its first great crisis centered in the death in February 1831 of Ellen Tucker. At twenty-eight, he faced then for the first time the shattering impact of a devastating grief. Five days after she died, he wrote in his diary: "This miserable apathy, I know, may wear off. I almost fear when it will. Old duties will present themselves with no more repulsive face. I shall go again among my friends with a tranquil countenance. Again I shall be amused, I shall stoop again to little hopes & fears and forget the graveyard. But will the dead be restored to me? . . . Shall I ever again be able to connect the face of outward nature, the mists of the morn, the star of eve, the flowers, and all poetry, with the heart and life of an enchanting friend? No. There is one birth & one baptism & one first love and the affections cannot keep their youth any more than men."

In his grief he turned with increased compulsion to brooding consideration of spirit. That was all that remained. Ellen had represented all of earthly loveliness:

> She who outshone all beauty yet knew not
> That she was beautiful, she who was fair
> After another mould than flesh & blood.
> Her beauty was of God—The maker's hand
> Yet rested in its work,
> And cast an atmosphere of sanctity
> Around her steps . . .
> Teaching that purity had yet a shrine,
> And that the innocent & affectionate thoughts

21

Ralph Waldo Emerson

That harbour in the bosom of a child
Might live embodied in a riper form,
And dwell with wisdom never bought by sin.

She who had been thus all things spiritual was spirit now. "Reunite us, O Father of our spirits," he prayed. What lived of her was spirit, and that was immortal: in that they might continue united. Emerson, brought face to face with death and the awesome mystery of death, saw beyond it to assurance of an immortality and centrality of spirit. He became increasingly assured that the "foundations of man are not in matter, but in spirit. But the element of spirit is eternity."

Hardly more than two weeks after Ellen's death, he was toying in his journal with such phrases as "God without can only be known by God within." Then for the first time he forthrightly articulated the certainty that has been described as the rock on which he thereafter based his life: "that the soul of man does not merely . . . contain a spark or drop or breath or voice of God; it *is* God." As Emerson now simply explained, "There is one light through a thousand stars. There is one Spirit through myriad mouths. . . . Every word of truth that is spoken by man's lips is from God. Every thought that is true is from God. . . . There is but one source of power—that is God." The still small voice to which man when he was very quiet or very tired might listen is not merely God speaking through man; it is God himself, the living word. "Man begins to hear a voice," he told his Boston congregation as he resigned his office of clergyman, "that fills the heaven and the earth, saying that God is within him."

Dwelling introspectively within himself, fed by sorrow, loneliness, and discouragement, he thus discovered God. Under the heading "Know Thyself" he explored and explained and rationalized his new discovery in verses that rush pell-mell in excited dogmatic, unabashed declaration

The Infinitude of the Private Man

that God did indeed dwell within him and within all people. A sense of unworthiness battles breathlessly with pride and excitement. He knows, he is certain, and the certainty is humbling, but exhilarating also. There is no placidity, no generous compromise in his voice now as he speaks, it has been said, as if ventriloquizing the words of the oracle:

> If thou canst bear
> Strong meat of simple truth
> . . . .
> Then take this fact into thy soul—
> God dwells in thee.
> . . . .
> Clouded & shrouded there doth sit
> The Infinite
> Embodied in a man.

It was a vaunting declaration, a challenge requiring not only recognition but response:

> Then bear thyself, O man
> Up to the scale & compass of thy guest
> . . . .
> Give up to thy soul—
> Let it have its way
> It is, I tell thee, God himself,
> The selfsame One that rules the Whole

and who "in thee resides," the selfsame "spirit that lives in all."

His voice rises then as if in inspired exaltation, firm in assurance, freed from bonds of inherited creed. He knew, and his knowledge demanded specific and instant exhortation:

> Therefore, O happy youth.
> Happy if thou dost know and love this truth,
> Thou art unto thyself a law
> And since the soul of things is in thee,
> Thou needest nothing out of thee,
> The law, the gospel, & the Providence

Ralph Waldo Emerson

Heaven, Hell, the Judgment, & the stores
Immeasurable of Truth and Good,
All these thou must find
Within thy single mind,
Or never find.
Thou art the *law*:
The *gospel* has no revelation
Of peace or hope until there is response
From the deep chambers of thy mind thereto
The rest is straw.

. . . .

Who approves thee doing right?
God in thee
Who condemns thee doing wrong?
God in thee
Who punishes thine evil deed?
God in thee
What is thine evil need?
Thy worse mind, with error blind
And more prone to evil
That is, the greater hiding of the God within.

And what of himself? "Shall I ask wealth or power of
God, who gave / As image of himself to be my soul?" The
asking was not necessary, for Emerson recognized the responsibility placed upon him by knowledge that he and all
others had immediate access to the spirit that mysteriously
controlled man and nature, a divine spirit that he shared,
and that he must freely share with all people.

As well might swelling Ocean ask a wave,
Or the starred firmament a dying coal
For that which is in me lives in the whole

Thus, born of insights bred of sorrow, Emerson's central
doctrine is set forth—the divine sufficiency of the individual
within whom dwells that which is eternal. It is well to recognize at once that this orientation throughout is religious.
Though he seldom went to church again—except to preach
—and later in life looked amiably toward what is called the
post-Christian era, he had a gospel of his own. "In all my

The Infinitude of the Private Man

lectures," he said many years later, "I have taught one doctrine, namely, the infinitude of the private man." For the rest of his life he preached possibilities—possibilities for heroism, for accomplishment, for progress, for insight into truth—of every single, separate person. "The individual," he explained, "has ceased to be regarded as a Part, and has come to be regarded as a Whole. He is the World." Again, he says, "The World is nothing, the man is all; in yourself is the law of all nature . . . ; in yourself slumbers the whole of Reason; it is for you to know all; it is for you to dare all." And again, "What can we see, read, acquire," he asked, "but ourselves." Humbly, he vowed,

> Henceforth, please God, forever I forego
> The yoke of men's opinions. I will be
> Light-hearted as a bird, and live with God.
> I find him in the bottom of my heart,
> I hear continually his voice within.

This certainty of the reality of an indwelling God would weave itself, implicitly or explicitly, through almost everything that Emerson thereafter wrote. When he explained it in greater detail in his essay on "The Over-Soul," people recognized it then as a modern restatement of the idea of emanation which had been developed by the Neoplatonic philosopher Plotinus some sixteen centuries before in Alexandria. The Over-Soul can be most simply explained as an infinitely great reservoir of spiritual power from which beams flow down into every individual person. It contains the truth of all truths, "within which every man's particular being is contained and made one with all others." For "within man is the soul of the whole; the wise silence; the universal beauty, to which every part and particle is equally related." Accessible to all persons, in many it is allowed to lie dormant. Many people habitually see the world piece by piece rather than as a whole. It is easier to depend on sense, prejudice, temper, or convention than to give oneself over to the truth discovered in one's own heart which when

25

Ralph Waldo Emerson

spoken correctly is recognized as truth by all persons because it enunciates what in their own hearts, unbeknownst before, is also true.

Recognition of this inflowing of truth must however be carefully guarded. Sensation can distort it: a sleepless night, illness of mind or body, a quarrel on which stands taken must be defended, the crippling of pain, or conventional requirements of decorum. Every person is somehow crippled, myopic, rheumatic, ridden by temper, driven by ambition—each plagued by conditions that may blur or place a veil between his recognition of the truth which is the God within. One must approach this God warily, certain that the approach has not been diverted by inherited assumptions, that the temple in which the God resides is a worthy dwelling. A person must watch his insights carefully to certify their authenticity.

But the God is there, waiting recognition. The possibility for prophecy is innate in every person who will submit himself to "that Over-Soul, within which every man's particular being is contained and made one with all others; that common heart of which all sincere conversation is the worship, to which all right action is submission; that over-powering reality which confutes our tricks and talents, and constrains every man to pass for what he is, and to speak from his character and not from his tongue, and which evermore tends to pass into our thought and hand and become wisdom and virtue and power and beauty."

These are heady words, meant to draw a person, if even for a moment, out of his workaday self toward recognition of infinite possibilities, never perhaps to be attained, but there for the taking when he will surrender himself to the commonality of divinity which he shares with all.

"Our age is retrospective," Emerson wrote in his first small book on *Nature*. It explains itself in terms borrowed from other people, of another time. Truth is dressed in worn garments patched to meet requirements of the present. We are slaves, he told students of the Harvard Divinity School,

26

The Infinitude of the Private Man

to revelations made by someone in the past. Are there not revelations to be made today? The world that surrounds us is filled with wonders. We must see that world for ourselves, and see it as if seeing for the first time, in fresh revelation. Let us lift from our backs the awful burden of the past.

"We see the world piece by piece," unknowing that the whole of which these pieces are but "shining parts, is the soul." And the soul, what is it to every person? "When it breathes through his intellect, it is genius; when it breathes through his will, it is virtue; when it flows through his affection, it is love," and "the heart which abandons itself to the Supreme Mind finds itself related to all its works, and will travel a royal road to particular knowledges and powers." Revelation is the "influx of the Divine mind into our mind. It is the ebb of the individual rivulet before the flowing surges of the sea of life."

Emerson spoke in the voice of his time. His confident assumption that what was true to himself in his own heart was inevitably true for all men anticipates the barbaric yawp of Walt Whitman who with equal confidence would vaunt, "I celebrate myself, / And what I assume you shall assume, / For every atom belonging to me as good belongs to you." It is possible to hear in Emerson the self-sufficient boast of the frontiersman or the self-congratulatory memoirs of the self-made captain of industry. His seems distinctively the voice of nineteenth-century America, of manifest destiny. He spoke what many men of his time who are now forgotten spoke, but he spoke it better. They were disputants, men of precise specification or of idealistic explanations unanchored to reality. Truth was available to them, but only by the artist is truth translatable: "We are all wise. The difference between persons is not in wisdom but in art."

Emerson was not a philosopher. To a large degree he simply rephrases what had often been said before. Nor was he a mystic sitting in silent meditation, consoling himself with beatified silent communion with the effluence of spirit. He was perhaps the most articulately realistic man of his generation. Reaching back, beyond the rationalistic Unitarianism of his day which seemed to say that all things could be explained by knowledge derived through the senses, he turned instead to an earlier pietism expressed by his Calvinistic forebears who claimed a "sense of the living presence of a power not our own before which man is nothing." He spoke much as Quakers had been persecuted for speaking. He talked now of much the same thing that Jonathan Edwards had talked of a hundred years earlier when he spoke of a "divine and supernatural light imparted to the soul by the spirit of God." The difference was that people like Edwards would allow recognition of this light only to a select few who had been chosen, elected by God for salvation. Emerson would extend to all men the ability to find God within themselves.

This was something that even his unfortunate brother Bulkeley could do, for recognition of truth did not depend on knowledge. It lay dormant in all people—those like Bulkeley, who did not develop mentally, as well as in his brilliant brothers who might have spoken bold truths. "The idiot, the Indian, the child and the unschooled farmer's boy," said Emerson, "stand nearer to the light by which nature is to be read, than the dissector or the antiquary." There are truths, that is, which come to man through other avenues than his senses, which transcend sense. That is something which William Faulkner, who shares with Emerson much of Protestant religious tradition, also talks about —in *The Sound and the Fury,* for example, where the idiot Benjy is as close to truth as is his brother Quentin, who goes to college and commits suicide, or his brother Jason, who does not go to college and seeks material wealth; it is set forth by Faulkner most tellingly in *The Bear,* where Ike McCaslin goes out to meet the mythical great beast which symbolizes something of primal power much as Moby-Dick does, and Ike cannot come upon or understand the bear

The Infinitude of the Private Man

until he has put behind him his compass, his watch, and his gun, accoutrements of civilization, the products of man's imperfect mind. It was a favorite notion of Emerson's time, adumbrated by Wordsworth in "The Idiot Boy," by Rousseau in *Emile*. It was among the primary injunctions of our founding fathers, who proclaimed that all men are created equal. It followed scriptures that talked of little children leading and of the impossibility of entering the kingdom of God without becoming as a child.

All people have equal access to God, which means that all people have equal access to truth. And this access has little to do with learning or wealth or inherited dogma. Emerson like many others of his time was in revolt against eighteenth-century rationalistic notions that all things could be measured quantitatively. With Jonathan Edwards he could ask, How large a thing is Truth? or Is Love round or square, hard or soft? There were truths that reached beyond what man could know through his senses or put together through the manipulation of what he had learned as one might put a jig-saw puzzle together. There was a method of apprehending truth that transcended sense or logic. People like Emerson who believed this were therefore called Transcendentalists.

Like most young men of his romantic—or perhaps any— generation, Emerson was in revolt against the past. He found the world as handed down to him an unsatisfactory world. Living at the latter end of a great revolutionary era, he shared with Rousseau and Jefferson and Thomas Paine something of the emerging nineteenth-century's faith in the individual man. Yet he distrusted the simple rationalism of these advocates of the social rights of man. He rebelled against the pervasive philosophy of John Locke, which was commonly interpreted as saying that all a man could know was what he learned through his senses. This put value on appearances rather than on that which was eternally true because shared by and accessible to all. Like his Puritan an-

Ralph Waldo Emerson

cestors, Emerson recognized the existence of truths derived from the inflowing spirit, the God who was in all people. There were truths that transcended experience.

The best way to get at Emerson is to come at him all at once, in the ninety-five pages of his little book called *Nature,* issued anonymously in 1836, which contains the compressed totality of all that he would subsequently patiently reveal. Revelation rather than logic was the instrument used by Emerson to delve toward truth. It was not his intention to create a philosophy or to codify thought. He distrusted logical arguments as man-made, and therefore inadequate because they are imperfect as man is imperfect. Neither philosopher nor conventional moralist, Emerson, it cannot be said too often, was first and last an artist who attempted to create a vision of the world and man's place in it. What is the world? What is nature which lies all about us? What is the refulgent beauty of nature that draws man out of himself, to quietness and calm, or to resolution? What are the mysteries of nature that inspired men resolve by conquering time or space through the discovery of such things as the telegraph, or the harnessing of waterpower and steam, or rocketing to the moon?

Not a philosopher, Emerson presented himself simply as a person who related what he had experienced, who revealed the world as it was revealed to him as he tried to see it fresh. He wrote as a realist writes. He had been there. He had seen. He knew. His essays, then, are not to be read as logical demonstrations, but as revelations. What truth is in them is not explicit, but implicit. They are to be read, that is to say, as poetry is read, not so much for what they say as for what they suggest of what cannot be said.

His sentences shimmer with meanings beyond logical explanation. The essay *Nature,* for example, has been described as not so much directly addressing the mind as using the "indirections of Nature itself upon the soul; the sunrise, the haze of autumn, the winter starlight seem interlocutors; the prevailing sense is that of an exposition in poetry; a high discourse, the voice of the speaker seems to breathe as much from the landscape as from his own breast; it is Nature communing with the seer."

There are three underlying ideas or postulates in this little book, but they are all-embracing. None of them is new with Emerson. He simply as artist expressed them better than many who had spoken them before. The first is the primacy of the soul, which is divine and identical in all men, a spark of eternity, presenting immediate access to all knowledge. It is the God, the all-prevailing spirit which is in all men. This certainty is expressed again as the first sentence of Emerson's remarks on "History" with which he introduced his first collection of *Essays* in 1841: "There is one mind common to all individual men," he said then very plainly. "Every man is an inlet to the same and to all of the same. What Plato has thought, he may think; what a saint has felt, he may feel; what at any time has befallen any man, he can understand. Who has access to this universal mind is a party to all that is or can be done, for this is the only and sovereign agent." He explains it more fully in his essay on "The Oversoul" in the same volume: "Man is a stream whose source is hidden. Our being is descending into us from we know not whence. . . . Let man then learn the revelation of all nature and all thought to his heart; thus, namely, that the Highest dwells with him; that the sources of nature are in his own mind, if the sentiment of Duty is there."

Notice the flick at the end of that last sentence—"if the sentiment of Duty is there." Emerson in *Nature* points to discipline as one of nature's great services to man. For all of what seem his attractive invitations to anarchy, Emerson continually pulls us up short, with insistence on man's responsibility, not only to eternity, but to his own time, on man's responsibility not only to himself, but to what is temporal also. Nature, he tells us, is everything which is not Me. The external world which is useful and beautiful, which makes it possible for us to create language and necessary for us to submit in discipline to its laws, which contains everything which we can hear, taste, touch, or smell or see, which includes our own bodies, flesh, blood, bone, and brain—this is nature. All besides is spirit, and it is this which all men share. What is our duty toward nature—what our duty to ourselves?

The second idea in the little book concerns the sufficiency of nature. Nature is the gigantic shadow of God cast on the senses. Nature is the image, the analogue of God. The beneficence, the beauty, the mystery of nature are like the beauty, the beneficence, and the mystery of God. It is a means by which God reveals his plan to man. What man sees in nature, however, is only partial truth, a shadow of the final truth that is there to be revealed when man can find it. Moses and Socrates, Ptolemy and Copernicus, Newton—and today he might add Einstein and many another—each has approximated truth, but the truth of one is discarded for the truth of the next, which will in its turn be discarded when another person pushes farther the boundaries of truth. The truth of which nature is thus the shadow has always existed in the mind of God. Man's quest is to discover and describe what portion of it he can. His materials are in nature, but the truth against which he may measure what he finds is in God, who is within man. The task is to see nature fresh, as the physicist does, the medical researcher, the jurist, or the poet, who sees beyond nature toward its increasing implications.

The ultimate function of nature, then, is to serve, to free the spirit, to unlock its capacities. It feeds us, pleases us, offers us images which we translate into words so that we may speak together, and its inexorable laws provide a discipline to which we at our peril fail to submit. But man is fed not that he shall eat, nor is he disciplined for discipline's sake, but that he may know the word which is with God. Nature exists, that is, solely for the use of spirit. Emerson never quite goes so far as to embrace idealism

The Infinitude of the Private Man

completely—to say that material things have no existence
except in the mind. What he does say is that they only
exist in anything approximating completeness as man recognizes them for what they are.

This imperfect, shortsighted, arthritic body of mine—to
take a very simple example—is but a shadow indeed of any
ideal of physical man; the blighted oak, the imperfect house,
the cumbersome bridge, and inadequately graded highway,
the poem that only streaks toward melody, or the experiment that approaches solution but just misses the mark,
these are images or shadows, metaphors of better things—
as when we say that God is like a father, or Jesus like a
lamb, or love like a red, red rose.

The third idea in the essay *Nature* derives from and might
even be thought of as a part or correlative of the first. It
concerns the immediacy of God. Deity, Emerson would tell
us, has "unrestricted access to every soul, and conversely
every soul has like access to all divinity, the process in
either case being a divine inflowing, not continuously felt,
but only in moments of exaltation such as can only be
self-certified, the mystic moments of a seemingly impersonal
or expanded being." As Emerson skirts close to pantheism,
which says that the universe is God, and as he toys momentarily with idealism also, so here he comes very close
to mysticism without becoming in any strict sense a mystic.
Emerson was not the kind of God-intoxicated man who, as
George Santayana has put it, "instead of perfecting human
nature . . . seeks to abolish it, instead of building a better
world . . . would undermine the foundations even of the
world, instead of developing our mind . . . would return it
to the condition of protoplasm—to the blessed consciousness
of Unutterable Reality."

Emerson's large value is that he was not this kind of a
world-renouncing mystic, but that he was a humanist, man-
centered in all of this thinking. "The flowering of civilization," he once said, is not society or any institution, but "is

33

the finished man, the man of sense, of grace, of accomplishment." But he recognized man as a God-reaching creature also; and he recognized, as almost everyone does, that there are certain rare moments in the lives of each of us, when we are very tired perhaps or excited or happy, when suddenly for a moment everything seems to fall into place. We become, in Emerson's words, "part or particle of God." We are nothing. We see all. The secrets even of all oracles seem answered. "A man should learn," Emerson tells us, "to detect and watch that gleam of light which flashes across his mind from within." We wish we had the power to recall those moments, to write them down, explain their revelation to us. Failing this, we turn in our inadequacy to the poets or the prophets, asking them to do it for us: "In every work of genius we recognize," Emerson reminds us, "our own rejected thoughts." These moments of insight are rare, but when they do come, we see truth for a moment face to face, not through the eyes of other men.

These three postulates—the primacy of the soul, the sufficiency of nature, and the immediacy of God—are the triple root from which grows Emerson's creation of the lineaments of the invisible world of spirit, which, because we are imperfect, is suggested to us through the imperfections of the physical world about us. In each of them is implicit Emerson's assurance of the divine sufficiency of the individual, of the opportunities for infinitude presented to the private man. The center from which all else radiates is the superlative value which he placed on "the unity of experience, the direct, momentary, individual act of consciousness." The trouble with most Americans, someone is said to have said, is that they die at thirty but aren't buried until they're seventy. Emerson pleads not only for the perceptive man whose senses remain alive so that he sees, but also for the man who will trust his perception to lead him independently to thought, who sees beyond things to meaning, to distinguish, as he puts it, facts amid appearances.

"A single thought," said Emerson in his "Natural History

of the Intellect," "has no limit in its value." "A rush of
thoughts," he wrote in his journal, "is the only conceivable
prosperity." Life is a quest for thoughts, a pursuit of inspirations. A single thought, one startling intuition can alter
the direction of all mankind. Man is born, he said, "to
sublimate the moment." Man's "whole possibility is contained in that habitual first look which he casts on all
objects."

One cannot understand any part of Emerson without
understanding the whole. When he insists in the opening
sentences of "Self-Reliance" that "To believe your own
thoughts, to believe that what is true for you in your own
private heart is true for all men—that is genius," he is
saying in another way only what we have been saying in
summarizing him—that the best in any person is the spirit
of that person, which is the inflowing spirit of God which
each person shares with all others; and that when any
person recognizes and expresses that spirit which is within
him, when he trusts himself and is true to his intuition, his
hunches, his own best beliefs, then what he says is true for
all people and is recognized by them as truth because it is
an expression of the same spirit which flows through them
also.

These challenging notions of Emerson's, as has been said,
were not new. The first thing to recognize about them, he
tells us in his essay on "The Transcendentalist," is that they
are "the very oldest of thoughts." That is what makes us
recognize them and their validity. They speak of something eternally true, which Plato described, and Plotinus,
Pythagoras, the scriptures of the Orient, the seventeenth-
century Puritan disputants, Coleridge, and Kant. They
speak of uncommon things in common phrases. They tell of
miracles—the miracle which is man, the bounteous miracle
which is nature, and the greatest miracle of all, "the perpetual openness of the human mind to new influx of light
and power . . . in inspiration, and in ecstasy." They counsel

Ralph Waldo Emerson

the highest and the loneliest kind of courage—to accept oneself "for better or worse as his own portion," to see for oneself, to recognize one's proper purpose, to discover the substance of his shrift, to "accept the place the divine providence has found for him in the society of his contemporaries," slave neither to that society which would mold him to its own faulty pattern nor to his own former opinions when he recognizes them false. They invite him to look to the God within, to listen carefully, and then to act: "A great soul will be strong to live, as well as strong to think. . . . Inaction is cowardice." We must "walk on our own feet . . . work with our own hands . . . speak our own minds."

This is heady counsel indeed. E. B. White once characterized Thoreau's winged words as 100-proof anchovy, too rich for much at a time; and the same is true of this man in whose footsteps Thoreau is said to have walked with steps painfully short. To Emerson God was not dead. He was present eternally within every person, waiting recognition. And Emerson is not dead; he exists as a constant prod, inciting each person to recognition of an ability to recognize truths that transcend learning and to rise to the highest plane that inherent individual disabilities allow. Perhaps the best advice that he gives in exhorting trust in ourselves is that we distrust him. Emerson is of the past. His words were directed to his generation, not ours. If we are Emersonian, we will refuse to go his way, but search out our own. We will not masquerade in his faded wardrobe, but pattern new garments with which to clothe the spirit. "The sun shines to-day also. . . . Let us demand our own words and laws and worship." That is the best of Emerson, that we must leave him behind. Our debt to him is ill paid unless we move from him toward something that neither he nor anyone else can give us, and that is the courage of our own, not his convictions.

III

Society and Solitude

H OW THEN is a person prisoned in society to build this world? To live independently, unshackled by contemporary opinion, is not difficult when a person is alone, when society does not command conformity, when the fluent opinions of other people do not entice. But society does impinge. How happy, said Emerson in his early essay on "Self-Reliance," is the response to the "voices which we hear in solitude, but they grow faint and inaudible as we enter the world. Society everywhere is in conspiracy against the manhood of every one of its members." Years later, writing of Montaigne, he admitted: "It is easy in the world to live after the world's opinions; it is easy in solitude to live after your own; but the great man is he who in the midst of the crowd keeps with perfect sweetness the independence of solitude."

One of the strands woven into the pattern of American thought is that of dogged nonconformity. As we began, so have we often remained a nation of rebels. But one of the strands woven with equal conspicuousness into the pattern of much American action is that of conformity. United we stand. The tensions resulting from conflicts between these two—the impulse to live outside of convention, to withdraw from society, as Thoreau did and as people do today who seek what seems to them a better, saner, more honest life-style than society requires, and the necessity of remaining within the confines of convention have been responsible for vigorous debate during our past 200 years. To what extent can an individual retain his individuality and yet remain a

Ralph Waldo Emerson

useful, contributing, cooperative member of the community? That, it has been said, is the central problem of a democracy. It is the artist's problem, the scholar's problem, the problem of any person of whatever age who is concerned with being his or her own self, acting according to his or her own persuasion. And it was Emerson's problem.

Nonconformity has been one of the hallmarks of the American experience. Sometimes it has surged to great, sometimes ridiculous, often frightening heights, in Emerson's time and in ours. At other times it has seemed quiescent or enfeebled into the kind of revolt that introduces only a new conformity, in a way of living, in dress, or in opinion. Emerson found his time enfeebled by conformity. The communes of his time, not unlike the communes of ours, seemed as much an escape from as a courageous confrontation of life.

The new United States was becoming prosperous as it stretched its arms greedily through the West and beyond the seas. Yankees were becoming thought of throughout the world as models of blackguard materialism, pious rogues who mouthed platitudes as they reached sticky fingers toward the public till. Round in belly, they had become flabby in spirit. "The mind of this country," Emerson told a Harvard audience in 1837, "taught to aim at low objects, eats upon itself. There is no work for any but the decorous, the complaisant." Public and private avarice have made us "timid, imitative, tame." The time has come, he challenged, "when the sluggard intellect of this continent will look out from under its iron lids and fill the postponed expectation of the world with something better than the exertions of mechanical skill."

Such words as these from his address on "The American Scholar" have been said to constitute America's intellectual declaration of independence. "Our day of dependence, our long apprenticeship to the learning of other lands draws to a close," he said. "The millions around us who are rushing into life, cannot always be fed on the sere remains of foreign harvests." The American must stand on his own two feet, think his own thoughts, act according to the dictates of his own conscience. The American scholar, who is any man who will think for himself, is "decent," he said, but also "indolent and complaisant." Approval is given only to those who will unthinkingly conform, who will think as their neighbors think, act as their neighbors act, and live sluggishly for the approval of people no less sluggish than they.

Emerson thus recognized the growth in America of what have been characterized as "outward directed" personalities, people whose actions, whose conventional vested suit, or whose carefully faded jeans, whose diction, whose prejudices and convictions, even the shaping of whose hair, are determined by the approval of their fellows. The result, then as now, is mediocrity—with my book-club selection as good as your book-club selection, my Mercedes or Volvo as good as your Mercedes or Volvo, my clothes as well cut or informally immaculate, my thoughts kept handily in deep freeze and packaged just about like yours.

"Is it not the chief disgrace of the world," Emerson asked, "not to be a unit; not to be considered one character; not to yield that peculiar fruit which each man was created to bear, but to be reckoned in the gross, in the hundred, or the thousand, of the party, the section to which we belong; and our opinions predicted geographically, as the north, or the south?" as when one says, All Yankees think this, all Southerners think that, all Californians are strange people indeed. If we walk on our own feet, work with our own hands, speak our own minds, then a "nation of men will for the first time exist, because each believes himself inspired by the Divine soul which also inspires all men."

No less than Thoreau, Emerson can be thought of as a man dangerous to many popular assumptions. He incites to rebellion. He requires careful inspection of what is and

Ralph Waldo Emerson

instant rejection of what should not be. A quiet man, he did not lead marches of protest. He seldom signed petitions. He did not advocate civil disobedience. He was in no ordinary sense a disrupter of peace, though he made giant onslaughts against the complacency that lulled his countrymen into a self-satisfied sense of security. Society held men in necessary bondage. Law was law, custom was custom, order was order, each man-made and necessary, but finally impediments. They were injunctions created by and for those people who, said his neighbor Thoreau, lived lives of quiet desperation, more interested in making a living than in living. Emerson recognized the attractive pitfalls of democratic capitalism. He knew both the necessity and the danger of being a good citizen. "The superior mind," he said in his essay on Montaigne, "will find itself equally at odds with the evils of society and with the projects that are offered to relieve them. The wise sceptic is a bad citizen; no conservative, he sees the selfishness of prosperity and the drowsiness of institutions. But neither is he fit to work with any democratic party that ever was constituted; for parties wish everyone committed, and he penetrates the popular patriotism."

Emerson was an indefatigable reformer, but he would not reform the world—he would reform man. Throughout, early and late, he continued to insist on each individual's responsibility: "To believe your own thought," secure in the belief "that what is true for you in your own heart is true for all men—that is genius." "Trust yourself," he commanded. "Whoso would be a man must be a nonconformist." "Nothing is at last sacred but the integrity of your own mind." "Insist on yourself; never imitate"—never imitate even yourself. "Nothing can bring you peace but yourself." Trust the thoughts that you think this day, rather than cuddling the thoughts you thought yesterday. It is with words like these, repeated often, that Emerson has become in all literature the supreme defender of the dignity of man, the inspiration of thoughtful men, and the comforter, it has been said, of all those who live in the spirit.

He spoke during a period when many reforms were astir, yet he asked only one reformation—that of the individual. The nineteenth century swarmed with earnest men and women who would reform society through better education, better diet, better living conditions. Abolitionists, teetotalers, vegetarians of every kind flourished. High-minded experimentalists flocked to the United States as to Mecca. Utopian communes were set up where men and women could live together according to superior plans, sharing work, sharing great thoughts, sometimes sharing wives. When Emerson's friend Bronson Alcott formed such a colony, he decreed that no one there resident should eat any but upward aspiring vegetables—only such things as beans and lettuce and asparagus; never onions, carrots, or potatoes. The reformers were numberless and varied, strong-minded and strange—like Carrie Nation, who attacked saloons with her hatchet, or Amelia Bloomer, who advocated the wearing of trousers by women. "Some," observed one contemporary, "had long hair, long heads, and long collars"; some even had "long ears."

These people were in the broadest sense socialists. They believed, as many people today believe, that if society can be reformed—even by law, by the abolition of slavery, the prohibition of alcohol, the banning of certain books—then each man in society will inevitably be better. Lift the mass, they said, and you lift the man. This was much the doctrine of such contemporaries of Emerson as John Greenleaf Whittier, William Lloyd Garrison, and Harriet Beecher Stowe.

Emerson's attitude was diametrically opposite. He had no faith in crusades, in reform movements, in organized charities, in mass activity of any kind. As remedies they were patchwork, a kind of jack-leg repair job that failed to get to the roots. Emerson was hardly in any sense of the word a socialist—though he has had the dubious distinction of being quoted with approbation in the *Daily Worker*. He was

Ralph Waldo Emerson

an individualist who said, let every individual recognize the best within himself and develop himself according to his highest capacities, and then it follows, as surely as night follows day, that the aggregate will be better also. Lift each person, he said, and the mass inevitably rises.

He distrusted organizations because they meant regimentation—just as Robert Frost seems to distrust them in "Mending Wall" and in his wonderful little poem about the ants who are so busy, so helpful one to the other, but so terribly departmental. An institution, said Emerson, in a sentence which is sometimes misapplied, is but "the lengthened shadow of a man." Not only must there first be a great man—a Jesus, a Socrates, a Calvin, a Thomas Jefferson, or a John Adams—to create a great institution, but that institution can only remain great when it produces the great men who will think freshly so that they can build upon rather than remain imprisoned within the framework which its founders laid.

But if Emerson were simply the advocate of radical individualism, he would not have been remembered any longer than have other men who have incited to anarchy. His attitude may seem unnecessarily austere, that an individual is inevitably diminished when forced to live with other men, that society binds him, customs chain him, and something of his inheritance of divinity is lost when he rubs elbows with his fellows. "Almost all people descend to meet," he tells us in his essay on "Friendship." "All association must be compromise, and, what is worst, the very flower and aroma of the flower of each of the beautiful natures disappears as they approach each other. What a perpetual disappointment," he said, "is society." It is "everywhere in conspiracy against the manhood of every one of its members. Society is a joint-stock company, in which the members agree, for the better securing of his bread to every stockholder, to surrender the liberty and culture of the eater. The virtue most in request is conformity."

Society and Solitude

He warns people who would be self-reliant to beware of the people whom they must meet, who are "deceived and deceiving." "Say to them, 'O father, O mother, O wife, O brother, O friend I have lived with you after appearances hitherto. Henceforth, I am to be truth's. Be it known now to you that henceforward I obey no law less than the eternal law. . . . I shall endeavour to nourish my parents, to support my family, to be the chaste husband of one wife—but these relations I must fill after a new and unprecedented way. I appeal from your custom. I must be myself." The individual is a society and a law to himself: "truly it demands something godlike in him who has cast off the common motives of humanity and has ventured to trust himself for a taskmaster." Emerson reacted against the early decades of the nineteenth century in much the same manner that T. S. Eliot reacted against the early decades of the twentieth, finding in them a wasteland society where men become "timorous, desponding whimperers." "Our housekeeping," said Emerson, "is mendicant, our arts, our occupations, our marriages, our religion we have not chosen, but society has chosen for us. We are parlor soldiers. We shun the rugged battle." He spoke bitterly of "the smooth mediocrity and squalid contentment of the times." In "The Sphinx" he describes the man of his time, who

> crouches and blushes,
>   Absconds and conceals;
> He creepeth and peepeth,
>   He falters and steals;
> Infirm, melancholy,
>   Jealous glancing around,
> An oaf, an accomplice,
>   He poisons the ground.

He looked with disdain on the "meek young men brought up in libraries," men who have been so weakened by patterns that they fear failure if they were to dare express themselves. Society is tinsel and froth and pretending. See,

45

he said, in contrast the backwoodsman, the frontiersman, who without book learning, disdaining convention, forages ahead in spite of hardship or rebuff, lands like a cat on his feet, relies on his own strength. A person of this kind is to be admired as strong, not squeamish, as capable of necessary harsh action on self-defensive aggression. He knows, as Emerson said in his essay on "Experience," that "Nature, as we know her, is no saint. . . . She comes eating and drinking and sinning. Her darlings, the great, the strong, the beautiful, . . . do not come out of Sunday School, nor weigh their food, nor punctually keep the commandments."

Emerson responded to hard, brisk incentives to action. He was fond of calling attention to the doubleness of things. It was man's fate to tempt schizophrenia by living on two levels, and there were—as has often been pointed out—two sides to Emerson: one idealistic, reaching for the stars; the other canny, and practical. James Russell Lowell early recognized the split in him when in *A Fable for Critics* he characterized Emerson as

A Greek head on right Yankee shoulders, whose range
Has Olympus for one pole, for t'other the Exchange.

He was both dreamer, that is, and a man of immense practicality. Some people have even discovered evidence of this doubleness in Emerson's features, which were slightly asymmetrical. Seen from one side, his face was that of the shrewd Yankee of tradition, calculating, serious, practical; seen from the other, it was that of a seer, a dreamer of dreams brooding on things to come, still far in the distance. Perhaps the best capsule characterization of Emerson was made by the French critic who called him an "enraptured Yankee." There was something to be said, he thought, for solitude; people needed solitude if they were quietly to reach. But there was much to be said for society also: to be isolated was to be sick. Society trained a person to practical temporal acquiescence, teaching him to live, not only within himself, but in harmonious relation with others. Too much mingling and a person becomes superficial, all surface, a polished veneer with no depth. To be too much alone, in self-absorption, breeds unproductive isolation. Emerson sought the more difficult middle life, perilous but exciting.

Emerson inhabits and invites us to inhabit a realm of spirit. But he was also a canny Yankee countryman, and he realized that there was a material world also, and that it was compulsively real. He knew that wood must be chopped and stacked if he and his family were to survive cold New England winters. He knew that his own frail physical body must be protected against the ravages of tuberculosis which had carried off his father and two of his brothers and his young wife. He knew indeed that there were truths which one recognized through contact with the material world, the world of the senses. And he delighted in plain, solid, substantial things: "I embrace the common. I explore and sit at the feet of the familiar, the low." "What do you really know the meaning of?" he asked. And he answered: "The meal in the firkin; the milk in the pan; the ballad in the street; the news of the boat; the glance of the eye; the form and gait of the body." "I confess to some pleasure," he said, "from the rattling oath . . . of a truckman or teamster." He recognized the efficacy of a good goddamn. "What a pity we cannot swear in society . . . for a hundred occasions," he said, "these forbidden words are the only good ones."

He recognized and he appreciated and he had a healthy respect for material things. "Nature," he said in his essay on "Fate," "is no sentimentalist,—does not cosset or pamper us. We must see that the world is rough and surly, and will not mind drowning a man or a woman. . . . The cold, inconsiderate of persons, tingles your blood, benumbs your feet, freezes a man like an apple. The diseases, the elements, fortune, gravity, lightning, respect no persons. The way of Providence is a little rude. The habit of the snake and

Ralph Waldo Emerson

spider, the snap of the tiger and other leapers and bloody jumpers, the cackle of the bones of his prey in the coils of the anaconda—these are in the system, and our habits are like theirs." Indeed, "Providence has a wild, rough, incalculable road to its end, and it is of no use to whitewash its huge, mixed instrumentalities, or dress up that tremendous benefactor in a clean shirt and white neckcloth of a student of divinity." Nature is "tyrannous circumstance, the thick skull, the sheathed snake, the ponderous, rock-like jaw." She is the tiger and the anaconda, of supple strength and irresistible cunning. She speaks what she means, no matter who mislikes the words.

Amid the terrors of nature, slave to mood and temperament, man depends, not on godlike sufficiency, but on the measure of skill or strength that destiny has allotted him. "When each comes forth from his mother's womb, the gate of gifts closes behind him." He has been created by circumstance: "he has but one fortune and that is already determined. . . . All the privilege and all the legislation in the world cannot meddle or help to make a poet or a prince of him." Sincerity was sorely tried as Emerson admitted, "I would gladly . . . allow the most to the will of man," even to lift himself above the mud and scum of things, "but I have set my heart on honesty . . . and I can see nothing at last, in success or failure, than more or less of vital force supplied from the Eternal. . . . The individual is always mistaken."

Against his assurance of the infinitude of the private man, we must therefore place his observation that "the key to all ages is imbecility; imbecility in the vast majority of men at all times, and even in heroes in all but certain moments; victims of gravity, custom, and fear." Waves of evil, he said, wash our institutions, and men in mass are "rude, lame, . . . narrow-brained, gin-drinking" nonentities, beyond rational assistance. "The worst of charity is that the lives you are asked to save are not worth preserving."

What then of the dignity of man about which we are

accustomed to hear Emerson so often speak? Even self-reliance can become "the goitre of egotism" and pretension, that foible, he says, especially of American youth. "The pest of society," he reminds us, "is egotists. There are dull and bright, sacred and profane, coarse and fine egotists. It is a disease that like mumps and measles fall on all constitutions." Blinded by mortality, disrupted by self-absorption, deafened by the clamor of the world, a coward cowering before the noise he helps to make, man beguiles himself with surfaces. "Our American has a bad name for superficialness," said Emerson. "Great nations have not been boasters and buffoons, but perceivers of the terror of life."

Baffled and bewildered, every honest man recognizes himself finally as a derelict. "It is unhappy, but too late to be helpful, the discovery we have made that we exist. That discovery is called the Fall of Man." On the evidence of phrases such as this, it is possible to nominate Emerson for a place beside Kierkegaard as one of the fathers of existentialism. "To Be," he said, "is the unsolved and unsolvable wonder," and to know a little, if one could be sure that he knew, "would be worth the expense of the world." But the cost of knowing is high: "People are not as light-hearted for it." Anxiety, perplexity, and gloom furrow the brows of thoughtful men.

The truths discovered through knowledge of these common things that Emerson, like every other person, knew and suffered and loved or feared, were recognized through his senses, through seeing them or hearing them or touching and smelling them. These were appearances that a person knew through experience, and was able to use or control through the exercise of what Emerson called his understanding. Understanding had to do with the picture of the world which man derived through the senses. And all combinations of knowledge which derive from observation —such things as time-tables, multiplication tables, systems

of logic, methods of bargaining, of political maneuvering—
these good and useful things, necessary things, were the
product of a person's understanding of what was to be
found in the material world, incentives to work and worry.

There were books about these things, and these books
were not to be disdained, for they were necessary books
which people in their quest for understanding must read
long and carefully. They taught useful skills—how to build
bridges, heal bodies, cook dinners, sell goods. Through them
one could learn how others had acted in other times. If they
were biographies, they could teach practical lessons of conduct or ways to wealth or power. If they were novels—and
Emerson did not disdain novels—they provided a vicarious
appreciation of people in situations similar to or excitingly
different from those of the reader. Books of this kind, on
this level—on the level of understanding—were in the truest
sense manuals that teach people how to manipulate things
about them, how to get along comfortably in the world,
how to make money, win friends, or live alone. They are
very important to people, because people live on this level—
that is why they are people. Understanding is very important, if a person is to nurture his physical needs.

But understanding leads to minor truths, which are
useful, but which are temporal and temporary. Truths like
this change day by day, year by year as fashions change,
as medical cures change, as man's ingenuity invents machines that ease or complicate his life. The world was in
essence no different after Galileo calculated that the sun
did not revolve about it, or after Robert Fulton put together
the steamboat. Examples multiply as we pass Emerson's
time and approach our own—do we write better with type-
writers, do we read better books under electric lights than
we did beside candles, is our horizon expanded or cluttered
by television? But we must not get off our point. One of
the most charmingly confusing results of reading Emerson or
talking about Emerson is—as I have already suggested—

that he gets us off his point and tempts us to explore not his thoughts of a century ago, but our own.

To Emerson and to people like him, understanding was not enough. It was useful and it was necessary; no person could get along very well without it—the multiplication table is a good thing to know, even when it can be proved through higher mathematics that two times two really does not make four; but the understanding does not explain everything. Emerson, as has been said, resisted John Locke's apparent insistence that all a person could know was learned through the senses. There were truths that sense could not reveal. The apprehension of these truths, said Emerson, was through the faculty of Reason—a word which he uses very differently from the way most empiricists use it today. Reason to him was that intuitive, in-dwelling faculty by which man recognizes truth and beauty and the kind of goodness which is something more than the adherence to man-made codes.

Reason belongs to every man, because within every man flows a portion of divine being. "Man is conscious," says Emerson, "of a universal soul within or behind his universal life, wherein, as in a firmament, the nature of Justice, Truth, Love, Freedom, arise and shine. This universal soul he calls Reason. It is not mine, or thine, or his, but we are its; we are its property and men." In one of those numerous capsule paragraphs in his journal, in which the whole of his thought seems to be explained in a few words, he explains: "Heaven is the name we give to the True State, the world of Reason, not of understanding; of the Real not the apparent. . . . It is, as Coleridge said, another world, but not to come. The world I describe is that where only the laws of the mind are known; the only economy of time is saying and doing nothing untrue to self."

People live, then, not only on the naturalistic plane of sensation. A person is more than the accumulated product of his experiences, more than the product of his environment. His actions are more than conditioned reflexes. His sensations, his experiences, his sensual apprehensions are real enough, and useful. For every natural fact—everything observed by any person in the material world, says Emerson —is a symbol of spiritual fact. Good fences, we can observe, do make good neighbors. It is really darkest just before the dawn, after the moon has set, before the sun has risen. These are facts which can be known through understanding, through patient observation. Yet each of them suggests something besides. Each points to a larger principle, a more universal truth.

To know spiritual truths, man turns not to manuals, to books that increase his understanding, not even, when he is best and strongest, to the observations of other men or even to the scriptures of mankind: he looks within himself. Within him is that portion of divinity that allows him to recognize truths that the senses cannot measure. And he knows that these truths that pass all understanding, discovered within himself, will when properly articulated be recognized as truths by all others, because each has equal access to the divine fount of truth. Recognition of the indwelling spirit is the tie that binds disparate selves, each a single and separate person, to assurance that the self is indeed divine. Heretical? Yes, in the eyes of many of Emerson's contemporaries, and dangerous also, as likely to mislead as to inform. Man must hold his guard high to defend himself against his self. Error, confusion, worldly self-seeking can distort recognition of the truth within. This has profound psychological and moral, and also literary implications.

There is a material world that one knows through the senses, through which one makes his way by the use of understanding. There is also a spiritual world, that man knows through the use of reason, intuition, insight. The material world is an imperfect copy of the world of spirit, and understanding is imperfect because it is a product of the imperfect mind of man. The truths of the material world are temporal, relative, partial revelations of eternal truths. Reason, which is an emanation of the mind of God, offers all people immediate access to truths that are eternal. Reason is found in solitude, understanding in the society. Both are necessary to a person doomed to live among other people if that person is to be whole. For whatever the divinity within, people are people, and imperfect. Reason is available, but at moments only, when a person can resist the necessary safeties of society.

Giving himself over to the elevating power of reason, a person may occupy "the whole space between God or pure mind and the multitude of uneducated men. He must draw from infinite reason, on the one side; and he must penetrate into the heart and sense of the crowd, on the other. From one, he must draw his strength; to the other he must owe his aim. The one yokes him to the real; the other, to the apparent. At one pole is Reason; at the other, Common Sense. If he be defective at either extreme of the scale, his philosophy will seem low and utilitarian, or it will appear too vague and indefinite for the uses of life." In his essay on "Montaigne" Emerson concludes: "Every man is related on the one side to sensation, and on the other to morals. The game of thought is, on the appearance of one of these two sides, to find the other: given the upper to find the under side. Nothing so thin but has these two faces, and when the observer has seen the obverse, he turns it over to see the reverse. Life is a pitching of pennies,—heads or tails. We never tire of this game, because there is still a slight shudder of astonishment at the exhibition of the other face, at the contrast of the two faces."

Emerson recognized the essential doubleness of things as they are revealed imperfectly to man. Man is damned with double consciousness, of the understanding and of the soul. The two "never meet and measure each other; one prevails now, all buzz and din; and the other prevails then, all infinitude and paradise." Man is disparate; unity exists only in the mind of God. To this man can reach in solitude; but he is only man, and imperfect, and he cannot always explain to other people what he has found there. His reading of nature is faulty so that the words he uses get in the way, clouding or discoloring truth. "It is the fault of our rhetoric," Emerson says, "that we cannot strongly state one fact without seeming to belie some other." He recognized that there "is often more communication in a touch or a glance than in the best wrought sentence."

Man in his inadequacy can only present as best he can first one, and then another, imperfect proximation, first one side and then the other—present dialectically first a thesis, then an antithesis. Crippled by his own abuses and by the abuses of society, he sees only in part. He can suggest but not provide the unifying synthesis. To him life remains inevitably a paradox. Truth, morality, justice, love—these are ambiguities and, as he fumbles to describe them, they reveal many meanings: this seems true and that seems true, and the two contradict each other. It is good to be alone, a self-reliant individual; it is good also, because it is necessary, to live among others. How then may man remain an individual and become at the same time a contributing member of society?

That, as we said at the beginning, is the question that Emerson asks. It is the question which any thinking man must ask: how much to yield, and when, and where? Emerson never answers the question, except by asking a dozen more. He presents this possibility, this alternative, the thesis and the antithesis, both partial, leaving the answer, the synthesis, which is beyond his power over words, to his reader. Perhaps, he seems to say, sometimes when you are very quiet or very happy or intellectually aroused, very deserving or very lucky, the answer will come to you, flashed from within. It is the "revelation of thought," he tells us, "which takes men out of servitude into freedom."

Society and Solitude

But these revelations of the God within are not easily transcribed.

By presenting both sides and insisting on doubleness, Emerson counsels against extremes. One who is alertly wise is neither so self-reliant that he becomes anarchist, nor so servile as to be bound to numbness by tendrils of society. "Solitude is naught, and society is naught. Alternate them and the good of each is seen." When a man "has sciatica in his loins and a cramp in his mind," he can yet find satisfaction in living within and, at the same time, living beyond the universe which benefits by his ruin: "The cold is inconsiderate of persons, tingles your blood, freezes a man like a dew drop. But learn to skate and the ice will give you a graceful, sweet, poetic motion. The cold will brace your limbs and brain for genius."

"Society and solitude are deceptive names," he concluded. A "sound mind will derive its principles from insight, . . . and will accept society as the natural element in which they are to be applied."

Man Thinking

IV

Books Are for Idle Hours

STRADDLING the horses of solitude and society, Emerson maintained a precarious balance, but the inside steed bore the greater portion of his weight. It trotted in shorter circles, less menaced by the circumscribing wall which society had built to keep each animal within bounds. It was nearer the center toward which, dismounting, the rider leaped. But Emerson dextrously avoided centrality. He preferred circles and circling. Quoting St. Augustine, he explained that "God is a circle whose center is everywhere and its circumference nowhere."

His best books are circular, their ends curving back to their beginnings, as in his first volume of *Essays* in 1841, which begins with "History"—"There is one mind common to all men. . . . Of the works of this mind history is the record," and then slyly in a useful pun, "This human mind made history, and this must read it"; then it ends with essays on "Intellect" and "Art," explaining in the first that "God enters by a private door to each individual," so that each may recognize truth when truly told, and in the second that it is the artist alone who can truly suggest to man the meanings and the opportunities of his story: "art should exhilarate, and throw down the walls of circumstance on every side, awakening in the beholder the same sense of exhilaration and power which the work evinced in the artist." And art is progressive in revelation: "its highest effect is to make new artists" who will each reveal his story truly. His story is history.

This story may be sought for in books, but books, though

Ralph Waldo Emerson

useful, are relics. They are repositories of the ideas or inspirations of other people. To the person who is awake to the moment, they are at best matters of the days gone by. Yet when Emerson startled his Harvard audience in 1837 by announcing in "The American Scholar" that books were useful only for that scholar's idle hours because they pinned him a victim to the past, he knew well that he expressed a partial truth. Books were important to Emerson. He was a prodigious reader of catholic taste. "Once," he said, "I took such delight in Montaigne that I thought I should not read another book; before that in Shakespeare, then in Plutarch, then in Plotinus; at one time in Bacon, afterwards in Goethe." He read avidly the writings of his contemporaries: Wordsworth seemed to him perhaps the greatest poet in English since Milton; Coleridge was a constant source of instruction and inspiration; Tennyson was mechanically melodious—"He has no wood notes"; Robert Burns was overrated; Dickens was a slight, exaggerating, fabulous showman, a master of "lively rattle, readable enough, and very quotable"; among novelists, Walter Scott was a favorite, read and reread. "I wish," he once told a lecture audience, "only to read that book it would have been a disaster to have omitted."

Books, explained Henry James, "did not feed" Emerson, "but they stimulated; they were not his meat but his wine—and he took them in sips. . . . He liked to taste but not to drink—least of all to become intoxicated." Better one's own thoughts than those which were spread before him by other people. "That book is best," said Emerson, "which puts me in a working mood." To him books were catalysts, useful in releasing or reaffirming his own insights. When he could not read nature, then a book was useful; it could for the moment nourish and sustain, suggesting new avenues toward inspiration: "Precisely in proportion to the depth of mind from which it issued, so high does it soar, so long does it sing."

That is one reason why Emerson is often difficult to

read. His books are catalysts that encourage disputation. He does not spread things out in logical order, for logic to him was a man-made device that shackles thought. Reading him, caught up by a single phrase or sentence, one's mind can begin to wander through thoughts of its own, leaving the trail which Emerson has cut for side-paths of its making. It becomes then itself an explorer through areas unrecognized before. Emerson is less likely to substantiate prejudices than to open doors that reveal new vistas.

"What's a book?" he asks himself in his journal. It is "everything or nothing. The eye that sees it is all. What is the heaven's majestical roof fretted with golden fire to one man, but a foul and pestilent contagion of vapors" to another. Sometime later he observed, "To an illiterate man, a book is only a collection of pages smutted over with black marks; to a boy, a goodly collection of words he can read; to a half-wise man, it is a lesson which he wholly accepts or wholly rejects; but a sage will see in it secrets yet unrevealed; shall weigh, as he reads, the author's mind; shall see the predominance of ideas which the writer could not extricate himself from, and oversee."

Each world that man inhabits has its own books. "History and exact science," Emerson reminds us, "he must learn by laborious reading. Colleges, in like manner, have their indispensable office,—to teach elements." But the wise man reads beyond the elements. His knowledge of historical or natural fact, his charts and tables of logarithms, his computers are gateways only. "Our science is sensual, and therefore superficial," our rules are subject to change, our rationalizings are built on inadequate premises. These things are of the world; on them the wise man broods, to them gives new arrangement. They are shadows, analogues, suggestions, metaphors of greater truths. He who can express that of which they are symbols is in the highest human sense a creator. He is the seer and sayer, both prophet and poet: "Nature offers all her creations to him as a picture language." He reads and translates, weaving his insight to new creation. "Bookman," he urged in a poem on mount "Monadnoc,"

> break this sloth urbane;
> A Greater spirit bids thee forth
> Than the gray dreams which thee detain.

"For the Universe has three children," writes Emerson in that superbly sacrilegious fourth paragraph of his essay on "The Poet." They are "born at one time" and they "reappear under different names in every system of thought, whether they be called cause, operation, and effect; or, more poetically, Jove, Pluto, Neptune; or, theologically, the Father, the Spirit, and the Son; but which we will call the Knower, the Doer, and the Sayer. These stand respectively for the love of truth, for the love of good, and for the love of beauty. These three are equal. Each of them is what he is essentially, so that he cannot be surmounted or analyzed, and each of these three has the powers of the others latent in him, and his own, patent." This we recognize as a trinitarian concept widely a favorite in the early nineteenth century. It is what Keats's Grecian urn suggested when it advised that beauty was truth, and truth, beauty. Poe said much the same thing, and Shelley, and Wordsworth.

"The poet," Emerson continues, "is the sayer, the namer, and represents beauty." His "being soars higher and sinks deeper than another's, to a softer tenderness, a holier ardor, a grander daring. This is the man who makes all other men seem less, the very naming of whose name is ornamental and like good news, and the sound of his words for ages makes the heart beat quicker, and the eye glisten, and fills the air with golden dreams." The poet sees beyond the world of matter to the essential relationship in harmony of all things: "For the world is not painted or adorned, but is from the beginning beautiful; and God hath not made some beautiful things, but Beauty is the creator of the universe."

Books Are for Idle Hours

The poet through language, which is analogy or metaphor, creates an approximation of the original creation. From disparate, conflicting elements of a world confused by multiplicity, he shapes an approximation of the unity which has always existed in the mind of God. "For poetry was all written before time was," and the poet with senses more finely perceptive than other men produces "transcripts, though imperfect."

The poet, the shaper or inventor, is man at his creative best, but is man still, and partial. He takes his place beside the lover of truth, the knower, and the lover of goodness, the doer, the man of moral action. These three partake of the qualities of one another, for "Words are also actions, and actions are a kind of words"—they sometimes speak louder and more effectively than words; and the poet himself becomes part of his poem because his moral character determines how clearly he will see, how distinctly he will speak; his is the voice of truth, but he can never utter the exquisite whole of truth, even as it is revealed to him. The poet, whether Shakespeare or Goethe or Byron, is scarred by worldliness. Partial himself, "he stands," Emerson explains, "among partial men," among other partial men, "for the complete man." He represents what he is; he exposes what no man foretold, but which all men recognize as their common wealth of truth.

> The gods talk in the breath of the woods
> And talk in the shaken pine,
> And fill the long reach of the old seashore
> With dialogue divine;
> And the poet who overhears
> Some random word they say
> Is the fated man of men
> Whom the ages must obey.

In placing the poet thus at the creative center, Emerson, says Stephen Whicher, "was being no more than true to his own experience; the poet was certainly *his* representative man." Emerson early thought of himself primarily as a poet. His essays, as has been said, must be read as poems are read, as much for what they suggest as for what they say. For more than twenty years he worked over a long, ultimately unfinished versified description of "The Poet," his possibilities, the pitfalls that menaced him, and his potentialities for pointing toward truths that belie appearances. This uncompleted poem is both an announcement of what an uncompleted Emerson would have liked to become and an uncompleted recognition of how difficult the task; it was a reminder to himself of the possibilities for redeeming power in poetry, but also of the muted power of his own verse.

For Emerson was often too cautiously self-controlled to be consistently a poet of the kind his requirements demanded. But he knew what poetry could be, and he valued it above all other forms of discourse. Though the absolute poetic life could perhaps never be realized, the poet's sense of the possibilities of such a life might of itself make him a liberating god. For all of his dislike of the jingling rhymes of Edgar Allan Poe, Emerson knew as well as he that "this / Is a world of sweets and sours," and that no mortal voice can tunefully reproduce the immortal melodies which, once sensed, tempt toward recreation.

Yet if one had a sense, however small, of what life at its best might be, duty compelled him to express that sense as best he could. For poetry commands a liberation of the intellect. "The poet's life is not a poetic life," it has been explained, "but an ascetic service to his thought. His reward, the reward he brings to others, is not self-union, but a magic flair of the imagination without means and without issue, an intoxicating glimpse of the inaccessible ideal." That is, the poet can bring to no person ultimate truth. No one can bring the perfect peace of total apprehension to a person, but the person himself. But the poet can incite or excite the imagination, so that the person can catch a momentary glimpse of truth or of the peace that passes all understanding.

"The great poet," Emerson says in his essay on the Over-Soul, "makes useful our own wealth." He does indeed dream an impossible dream, attempting to, but never quite succeeding in, catching it up within the skein of words. "Oh Poet!" Emerson wrote in his journal in 1838, "thou wert ten times the poet, if thou couldst articulate the unsaid part." Pragmatically, the imaginative insight of the poet at his best stimulates in the reader or the listener an insight approximate to that of the poet's—which is much what T. S. Eliot meant when he spoke of the objective correlative. The poet does not say: he suggests. When the reader responds, then poetry is born.

Poetry, which inspires by indirection, can only be defined by indirection. The "uncontrollable interior impulse which is the authentic mark of a new poem . . . is unanalyzable," said Emerson. It is "the perpetual endeavor to express the spirit of the thing." It "teaches the enormous force of a few words." A "true poem is the poet's mind," for poetry "is the only verity—the expression of a sound mind, speaking after the ideal and not after the apparent." He would have agreed with Martin Heidegger, who said a century later, "Poets are the mortals who . . . sense the trace of the fugitive Gods," and utter what is holy. God himself, Emerson once said, "does not speak in prose, but communicates with us by hints, omens, inferences." Poetry is not confined by rule or regulation or man-made inventions of form. Its substance creates its own form, inevitably different from any other: "It is not metre, but metre-making argument that makes a poem." Pondering long on the mystery of poetry, Emerson finally admitted, "the secret of poetry is never explained— It is always new. We have not got any farther than a mere wonder at the delicacy of the touch and the eternity it inhabits." At best, it fumbles toward what cannot be expressed.

Ralph Waldo Emerson

Throughout much of his life, Emerson thought of himself as a poet who might indeed rename the beasts of the fields and the gods of the sky. But he was humble in his pretensions. "I am a born poet,—of a low class without doubt," he admitted, "yet a poet. That is my nature and vocation. My singing, to be sure, is very husky, and it is for the most part prose. Still I am a poet in the sense of a perceiver and dear lover of the harmonies that are in the soul and in matter, and especially of the harmonies between these and those." This was the voice of the early Emerson who in the mid-1830s stood on the verge of his career. Some twenty years later, disappointed at the reception of his verse, he deplored that "owing to my sad lack of fluency, my poems have seemed almost to fall dead. My prose has served to keep up a little interest in them, but I think they are scarcely known at all. It appears rather a hard thing to me that I should be so lacking in the faculty, which in others delights me more than anything. How charming this fluency which many of our poets seem to have!" But fluency, however attractive, was not the ideal. Tennyson was fluent, he said, "But I seldom read him now. . . . I prefer to go to the original strong poetic spirit, even expressed in crude words." Condensation was what was wanted, and fresh insight which was revelation unforetold. Yet Emerson's poetry, once undervalued, considered harsh and strange by his generation, is now better appreciated. "One who knows the poetry" of Emerson, said Robert Frost, "hardly needs to read the prose."

Emerson's poems are indeed often brief and condensed rehearsals of or afterpieces of his essays, in some respects so succinctly epitomized that they defy precise explication. Yet Emerson has been recently identified as the fount from which much of the best of subsequent American poetry has derived. He has been called the masculine voice of New England, as Emily Dickinson was the feminine voice. Along with Melville and Thoreau and Whitman, far more than Longfellow or Lowell or even the occasionally gifted folk-poet Whittier, Emerson performed in verse and prose the function of the poet. In revolt, not only against the established, but against the insincere, the glib, the imitative, like Ezra Pound a century later, Emerson admonished against repeating in borrowed measure what hundreds of other poets had said before. His verse struggled to free itself from the ornamental excesses in which much Victorian verse is smothered. What needed to be said needed no embellishment.

His verses are often rough. He is said to have been tone-deaf, so that his poetry, like the near-blind prose of James Joyce or the near-blind drawings of James Thurber, often because of hindrance achieves a quality of its own, like "the robe of a monarch," said Oliver Wendell Holmes, "patched by a New England housewife." He is supposed sometimes purposely to have roughened his verses, to startle a reader, to discover unexplored avenues toward insight. He disliked verse, like that of Tennyson or Poe, which lulled in hypnotic rhythms which wrapped truth in attractively disguising garments. Verse of this kind, he said, was fit only "to put around a frosted cake"—sweet, but not nourishing. Truth should be naked, unashamed of what is revealed.

His formal essays on poetry and poetics, such as "The Poet," "Poetry and Imagination," "Shakespeare; or, the Poet," and "Persian Poetry," and his observations on poetry scattered through other essays and in his journals and letters, although highly individual and freshly perceptive in phrasing, are discovered to be a blend of theories of Platonism and Oriental thought, with echoes of Elizabethan and seventeenth-century practice, and especially of late eighteenth-century aesthetics as set forth most effectively, he thought, by Coleridge. Emerson is unashamedly eclectic. He read widely in other men's poetry, often divergent in theory and practice. He sets forth, as has been said, no easily definable, consistent theory of his own, only hints or examples of what poetry can be. He refuses to dim by the false light of definition that which is undefinable.

Ralph Waldo Emerson

Yet there has been a persistent temptation to systematize Emerson, to translate him to commonalities. His statements on poetry have been categorized into neat pigeonholes, but as each is filled, it spills over into the next, because Emerson is not, it cannot too often be said, a consecutive thinker. He defies attempts to define him, as philosopher or poet. Matthew Arnold came close to identification when he called him "the friend and aider of those who live in the spirit."

There are, however, some things which can be suggested about Emerson's attitudes toward poetry. I shall venture three. In the first place, he was man-centered, a humanist. As such, he is not so much concerned with people as they are, which approximates realism; nor in people as worse than they are, which suggests certain elements of naturalism; nor in people as they wish they might be, which is one of the aspects of romanticism; but in people as they ought to be, capable of being led toward the highest and best of the human potential, and this was to Emerson recognition of the infinitude of every person who will submit to guidance by the God within. Emerson stands with Milton and Shelley and all humanists everywhere in insisting on the high and sacred office of the poet who "stands among partial men for the complete man," with responsibilities for revelations perhaps beyond what his skill can communicate.

Insofar as his perception is dulled even by small immoralities or minor inadequacies, whether physical or of the spirit, by so much is the poet disqualified from seeing clearly. When Emerson's tone-deafness or color-blindness or his concern with health got in the way to distort his perception, even of external things, he was to this extent less a poet. The flaw among all poets, whether Byron, Goethe, Wordsworth, or Shakespeare, was, he thought, a moral flaw that clouds perception or that tempts to the creation of images that reflect temporal rather than eternal truths. That was the rock, I think he would have said, on which Poe and Hart Crane, Baudelaire and Dylan Thomas, to name but four, each floundered. The discipline demanded of the poet is greater than the poet, being man, can bear; yet it is demanded of him and it isolates him from other persons who are satisfied with less. The sacrifice must be made, if the poet is, as Emerson says, to see and handle that of which others dream, if he is to announce what no man foretold.

To apprehend, then to communicate beauty, which is the harmony and wholeness of the universe, the secret that man can never understand but only know, this is the poet's role. To see nature clearly as it is revealed today, his senses fresh, as unscarred as possible by worldliness—is his first task; to discover within himself the revelation that is all truth—is the second: to be, as Emerson wished to be, "a perceiver and dear lover of the harmonies that are in the soul and in matter, and specially of the harmonies between these and those"—to find words, images, analogues based upon nature that man may understand in order to articulate the revelation.

For Emerson shared with others of his time the belief that poetry is mystery, that it is the result of inspiration; and that it cannot be coerced. It comes on the poet unawares, and he must seize it quickly before it passes. Neither intellect nor logic can lure it. No pretold, man-made scheme can hold it. It is sudden. It is inconsecutive. Health, rest, human intercourse, solitude of habit, life in the open, study —all these, we are told in *Nature* and "The American Scholar," are favoring circumstances which in the right proportion may allow the poet to make the unseen visible by means of language. Neither self-conscious nor society-conscious, the poet is admitted to truth without the penalty of understanding. Because he tells what no man foretold in a manner for which no previous pattern has existed, the poet is unshackled and untamed. He "speaks adequately," says Emerson, "only when he speaks somewhat wildly," as

Ralph Waldo Emerson

Poe's angel Israfel spoke "wildly well" because his heart-strings were a lute upon which were played melodies that were immortal.

Emerson best suggests his meaning when he puts it in poetry—as when in "The Problem" he explains that

> The litanies of nations came,
> Like the volcano's tongue of flame,
> Up from the burning cores below,
> The canticles of love and woe

or when he says of the inspired architect of St. Peter's in Rome:

> He builded better than he knew;
> The conscious stone to beauty grew.

And in his poem "Bacchus" he yearns for "wine which never grew / In the belly of the grape," which, drinking, will allow him to hear "far Chaos talk with me; / Kings unborn shall walk with me; / And the poor grass shall plot and plan / What it will do when it is man." In one of his longer poems, "Merlin," he attempts once more to suggest what a poem at best can be.

> The trivial harp will never please
> Or fill my craving ear;
> Its chords should ring as rings the breeze,
> Free, peremptory, clear.
> No jingling serenader's art,
> Nor tinkle of piano strings,
> Can make the wild blood start
> In its mystic springs.
> The kingly bard
> Must smite the chords rudely and hard,
> As with hammer or with mace;
> That they may render back
> Awful thunder, which conveys
> Secrets of the solar track,
> Sparks of supersolar blaze.
> Merlin's blows are strokes of fate,

Books Are for Idle Hours

Chiming with the forest tone,
When boughs buffet boughs in the wood;
Chiming with the gasp and moan
Of the ice-imprisoned flood;
With the pulse of manly hearts;
With the voice of orators;
With the din of city arts;
With the cannonade of wars;
With the marches of the brave;
And the prayers of might from martyr's cave.

This is rather more explanation, perhaps, than poetry. But it is strong and free in content and manner. It recalls Walt Whitman, who thrilled to respond to Emerson's challenge. It echoes John Keats's "A drainless shower of light is poesy; / Tis might half resting on its own right arm"; or the Irish poet's boast that "the poet is a brave man with a sword." As Emerson writes further of Merlin, he says:

Great is the art
Great be the manners of the bard.
He shall not his brain encumber
With the coil of rhythm and number;
But, leaving rule and pale forethought,
He shall aye climb
For his rhyme,

and "mount to paradise / By the stairway of surprise."

This anticipates my third observation on Emerson's conception of poetry. It is centered in his statement, already quoted in part, that "it is not metres, but metre-making argument that makes a poem,—a thought so passionate and alive that like the spirit of a plant or animal it has an architecture of its own, and adorns nature like a new thing." He wants "no men of talents who sing," but "stout-hearted forgers of song": "Talent," he says, "may frolic and juggle; genius realizes and adds." What there is of structure, of unity, or of meaning exists, not because of conventional pattern or pretty phrasings which man may learn as a higher

71

Ralph Waldo Emerson

alphabet, but in the organic and original form, the intrinsic unity, the irrepressible and inevitable words into which the poem naturally flows. How inconsequential are the conventional trappings of poetry, like rhyme and lilting rhythm! How fragile the delicately wrought jars of form—the sonnet, the quatrain, the intricate stanzas of the virtuoso—into which man has been taught to confine his thought, as if thought or beauty could be poured to a mold! Thought, perception, beauty which is its own excuse for being, must be free to soar or sink wherever the free-ranging insight of the poet leads. It can and will and must create its own form.

The effect of thoughts like these on the literature of our own day is immediately evident—in free verse and in the kind of episodic short stories we have become familiar with in contemporary periodicals. Not only our literature, but modern architecture and the plastic and the visual arts, and music, also, have felt their impact. Emerson was of course not the originator of ideas such as these. The principles of organic unity of the kind for which he called had been set forth often before his time, and in his time by the Schlegels in Germany and, for him most effectively, by Coleridge who summed up the central idea which Emerson expounded: that genius cannot and must not be lawless, but that it must avoid mechanical or predetermined form and insist upon a form of its own which is innate in the subject and which "shapes as it develops, itself from within," so that its form is natural rather than geometric, grows to a unique configuration of its own, like that of a tree, or the life of a person.

"Ask the fact for the form," said Emerson. Structure no more than thought can be retrospective. Form is not determined by classical unities nor by neoclassic rules of art, but is created each time anew by the artist. Structure is the servant of function. The material of art is nature in which the artist discovers symbols of eternal truth. The beautiful therefore is useful, meant not just to please, but to be beneficial to and instruct man. The tendency in artificial societies is to create an artificial art which obscures the functional in trivial and effeminate ornamentation. A poem, a great drama, or a fine building creates its own form, which depends on its function, what of usefulness it is intended to provide. Form thus creates meaning. Ornamentation for its own sake was trivial, whether in rhymes which jingle or in rococo decoration in architecture: "outside embellishment," said Emerson, "is deformity. . . . Our taste in building refuses pilasters and columns which support nothing, and allows the real supporters of the house to show themselves."

Art should be inevitable. Emerson approved the sentiments of his architect friend Horatio Greenough, who said, "Let us begin from the heart as a nucleus and work outwards." Art exists neither as the medium for the exhibition of the talents of little men nor as "their asylum from the evils of life." One does not, as Robert Frost once put it, escape from life in poetry, but escapes into life, to essential reality. In art, in poetry specifically, man can create only an approximation of the intention of the supreme artist-creator, whose truth is beauty, and whose beauty is truth and goodness. Finding in natural facts symbols of divine fact, a person, when poet, creates images which suggest the perfect harmony that exists and has always existed in the mind of God. The poet, through his fumbling to say what cannot be said, stimulates those who are less perceptive, less articulate. "Our music, our poetry, our language itself are not satisfactions, but suggestions." The poet "smites me and arouses me . . . breaks up my whole chain of habits," says Emerson, "and I open my eye on my own possibilities." For the use of poetry, as of all of literature, is "to afford us a platform whence we may command a view of our present life, a purchase by which we may be moved."

Essentially and inevitably, each person, however mute, is poet when he dares to recognize the God within, to probe beyond appearances, in confidence to discard derived opinion. Books are for idle hours, which are many because people may cling to idleness as defense against themselves and the sometimes troublesome world which offers itself for their discovery. Books thrill and instruct and inspire, and people, being partial, cannot do without them. But, warns Emerson, "books approach very slowly the things we wish to know." When, as only occasionally, one can listen to the voice of the God within or find in nature symbolic manifestations of truths yet untold, then books, all books, even the Book, are useful only as reminders of what has been or inciters toward fresh revelation which comes, not from the book, but from the impetus it supplies: "The great poet makes us feel our own wealth."

These are heady admonitions, grounded in faith, certified by experience. Their assurance of the inherent right to independence, their assumption that each person is an individual self, capable of confidence in the correctness of his own best thought, fit well with the exuberant spirit of Emerson's time, and perhaps of ours. But they were also self-defending, insisting that, though trial was required, intention did not insure accomplishment. To see was not inevitably to say. For Emerson recognized himself as a partial man, crippled like all others by innate or imposed disabilities. In his own verse he seldom achieved the wildness which he advocated, or the freedom of form. His best-remembered poems like "The Concord Hymn" and "The Humble-Bee" are conventional in rhyme and meter. Perhaps because it is early, his poem which begins "Good-bye, proud world! I'm going home" is filled with commonplace echoes. "Uriel," "Bacchus," and "The Sphinx" are puzzle poems, on the implications of which few serious readers agree. Other frequently anthologized poems, such as "Give All to Love," "The Problem," and "Each and All," are superior in parts but unsatisfying as poems impeccably complete. There is often a forced quality in Emerson's rhyming which gives the impression that the poet, though attempting to say unusual things, distorts them through submission to convention. He sometimes seems to be like his "patient Pan," who,

Books Are for Idle Hours

"Drunken with nectar, / Sleeps or feigns slumber / Drowsily humming / Music to the march of time." In prose adventuresome, in verse Emerson was often timorous, as when in "Grace" he confesses;

> How much, preventing God, how much I owe
> To the defenses thou has round me set;
> Example, custom, fear, occasion slow,—
> These scorned bondmen were my parapet,
> I dare not peep over this parapet
> To gauge with glance the roaring gulf below,
> The depths of sin to which I had descended,
> Had not these me against myself defended.

He seems to be fearful of the power of poetry, fearful perhaps that he could not sound its depths unscathed. He had the vision, it has been said, but not the voice, the unerring voice. When late in life he put together an anthology of poetry called *Parnassus,* in its preface he expressed somewhat more specifically what he had intimated often before: "The poet," he said, "demands all gifts, and not one or two only"; he "must only converse with pure thought, but he must demonstrate it almost to the senses. His words must be pictures: his verses must be spheres and cubes, to be seen and handled."

For all their occasional excellence in part, few of Emerson's poems can be appreciated except with sympathetic understanding of what he hoped they might have been. Few of them have the coordinated toughness that protects and preserves a great poem, however it is mauled or mishandled by attempts at interpretation. Though it has been thought to speak of other things besides, perhaps his fine poem on "Days" speaks also of his disappointment in himself as a poet:

> Daughters of Time, the hypocritic Days,
> Muffled and dumb like barefoot dervishes,
> And marching single in an endless file,
> Bring diadems and fagots in their hands.

Ralph Waldo Emerson

To each they offer gifts after his will,
Bread, kingdoms, stars, and skies that holds them all.
I, in my pleached garden, watched the pomp,
Forgot my morning wishes, hastily
Took a few herbs and apples, and the Day
Turned and departed silent. I, too late,
Under her silent fillet saw the scorn.

His best poetry was in his prose, which though seemingly didactic, played a multitude of changes upon a single familiar theme.

V

The Invariable Mark of Wisdom

A ND PROSE, no more than verse, was not to be con-
trived. When effective it is natural, spontaneous,
allowing the subject to create the form. Emerson denied
distinction between what were called the fine and the
useful arts: "In nature all is useful, all is beautiful," because "it is alive, moving, reproductive, . . . symmetrical
and fair." He admired the "frolic architecture of the snow,"
windblown to forms of unanticipated natural beauty. He
discovered that "more exquisite art goes into the formation
of the strawberry than in the costliest palace that human
pride has ever reared." The artist must look to these things,
for art is deeply rooted in nature, even in its most ordinary
aspects: "The invariable mark of wisdom is to see the
miraculous in the common."

When in "The American Scholar" Emerson asserted that
he embraced the common, and explored and sat at the feet
of the familiar, the low, he was more than paying lip-service
to Wordsworth's famous pronouncement in the introduction
to *Lyrical Ballads* that in "low and rustic life . . . the
essential passions of the heart find a better soil in which
they can attain their maturity, are less under restraint, and
speak a plainer and more emphatic language; because . . .
elementary feelings exist in a state of greater simplicity."
Emerson is only saying in another way something he had
said before and which he would say again: that "the world
exists for the education of man," and that every natural
fact is symbol of spiritual fact, so that everything perceived
or learned has meaning which transcends itself if a person

79

Ralph Waldo Emerson

has wit to recognize it. Emerson would find his subjects, he said, in "the meal in the firkin; the milk in the pan; the ballad in the street . . . the shop, the plough, the ledger" because in these things were hidden the secret of all life. "There is no trifle" which rightfully recognized is not unified and animated by a design of its own.

"The trivial experience of every day is always verifying some old prediction to us," he said again. "A man leading a horse to water, a farmer sowing seed, the labor of haymakers in the field, the carpenter building a ship, the smith at his forge, or whatever useful labor, is becoming to the wise eye." The sound of "rats in the wall," the sight of "the lizard on the fence, the fungus under foot, the lichen on the log" are reminders to man of how little he knows "sympathetically, morally of either of these worlds of life." The wonder of the egg, the grub, the caterpillar, the fly—all different, but one individual—reminds him of unity to be discovered in other seemingly disparate things. "Nature is a mutable cloud which is always and never the same. She casts the same thoughts into troops of forms." It is through experience, through perceptive observation of things about him that man approaches truth. George Santayana described Emerson as one who "opened his eyes on the world every morning with a fresh sincerity." He wished to see all things as they really were. Coveting truth, he returned daily to experience. "Give me insight into to-day," he said, "and you may have the antique and the future worlds."

Today for Emerson meant aspiring young America, swelling swiftly westward; it meant the democratic aspirations of the new world; it meant the reachings toward fresh perfections of his idealistic contemporaries; but it meant also the helter-skelter rush of life in market, seaport, farm, and frontier. Recognizing this, he admonished, "If you would learn to write, 'tis in the street you must learn it. Both for the vehicle and the aims of the fine arts you must frequent the public square. The people, and not the college, is the writer's home." Not all things will be pleasant there:

The Invariable Mark of Wisdom

"I see the disappointed man in whom every prospect fails; I see lonely and unhappy women, I see age left childless and the invalid of many years. I see the repressed debtor, the suspected, the friendliness and the mourner." But life was there, and possibilities; even among the muck of things, was nature, raw, merciless, holding forth gifts, but ruthless in exacting toll, scornful of those who refused its offerings.

For America was more than a country with physical potentialities which seemed boundless; it was compounded of ideals of liberty, democracy, and equality exemplified in the activities of its teeming millions. Recognition of the potentialities of America wove itself like a golden thread through the pattern of Emerson's thought. "America," he said, "is the idea of emancipation." Among other things, it was, as he had said, emancipation from dead ideas of the past; specifically, it was emancipation from the hold that Europe, her manners and her literature, held over the infant republic. "Can we never extract this tape-worm of Europe from the brain of our countrymen?" he asked in his essay on "Culture." He hoped that "one day we shall cast out the passion for Europe by the passion for America."

It was in response to thoughts like these—expressed often before Emerson's time, but expressed by him for his time— that people like Walt Whitman arose to sing America or to hear, as Whitman put it, America singing. The kind of particularization, of focussing on the present fact of everyday life which Emerson called for (and, as has often been pointed out, he could not himself always achieve in his own writing) was what Whitman imitated and expanded as he wrote of the sights and sounds, the occupations and the shortcomings and the well-meaning assurance of American people. Emerson encouraged men like Thoreau to reach for secrets of the universe in examining nature as it existed in wood lots and meadows close about them. One needed no excursion to Egypt to read the riddle of the Sphinx. The answer was anywhere where perceptive man could find it. But it was, Emerson suggested, in the most completely emancipated portions of the new world, like the frontier, where the surest substance for her literature lay. "Our eyes," he said, "will be turned westward, and a new and stronger tone of literature will result. The Kentucky stump-oratory, the exploits of Boone and Davy Crockett, the journals of western pioneers, agriculturalists, and socialists, and the letters of [the humorist] Jack Downing"—these to him were "genuine growths." These were sought out and admired even in Europe or by people from Europe, "where our Europe-like books are of no value."

This was a patriotic theme, and Emerson as a man of his time sounded it again and again, in repeated assertions of literary independence; it was nationalistic, but it represented also a kind of higher patriotism, loyalty not to a nation which Emerson found in many respects far from ideal. Its loyalty was to the spirit of its people who grasped firmly the fresh revelations of a fresh new world, and who recognized the potentialities of that spirit. Man, not nation, was the measure of all things. Truth discovered today, not regulations inherited in constitutions or creeds—that was to be sought.

Idealistic and optimistic, it was at the same time the most practical of quests. An inbred Yankee realism kept Emerson in touch with the actualities of his own time and place. Though he dreamed of a future and better America, he also recognized and outspokenly exposed the failures and the shortcomings of his own time. He has been called the "great American mediator," and this is in large part true. Both idealistic and often surprisingly practical, requiring intellect but demanding insight, a disciple of nineteenth-century buoyant optimism but dedicated as well to a disciplined, inherited morality, responding to the democratic dream of possibilities for America but finding comfort in cultural ideals borrowed from Europe and the Orient, he often merely described these alternatives, suggesting grounds for their reconciliation.

The Invariable Mark of Wisdom

His realism, his insistence on concentrating on the demands of the present, was partly an inherited Yankee trait, based on the pragmatic common sense of what we would now call "know-how"—like the famous epigram of the man who built the better mousetrap. It is exemplified in his admiration for the Irish servant girl who could manage his balky cow better than he could merely by slipping her finger under its tongue. But his realism was philosophic also. He respected tools because they were instrumental to an understanding of reality. Common sense things of the world were reflections of a higher universal sense. They were excellent insofar as they fit to a utilitarian pattern which was itself excellent as suggestive of the harmonious pattern of the universe as it exists in the mind of God. Thus, Emerson, among other things, has been recognized as a precursor or early exponent of pragmatism, who contributed to the later formation of that philosophy by William James and John Dewey.

"Let the scholar first learn things," said Emerson. Let him be sure of and accumulate his facts. Speaking not only of the scholar but of every person, he again admonished, "Let him know how the thing stands; in the use of all means, and most in the reverence of the humble commerce and humble needs of life,—to hearken to what *they* say, and so, by mutual reaction of thought and life, to make thought solid and life wise." When William James read these words in Emerson's essay on "The Method of Nature," he noted in the margin of his copy that this was pragmatism. The "mutual relation of thought and life" was a theme common to Emerson and these later, more explicit explainers of people's relation to the world. "I love the music of the water-wheel," said Emerson; "I value the railway; I feel the pride which the sight of a ship inspires; I look on trade and every craft as education also."

"But let me discriminate," he said, "what is precious herein." It is the act of invention or creation, that had made possible these things that he admired, not the mechanical routine which maintained them; that initial act was a spiritual act, it was a seizing on a perception of the moment. It was a pragmatic utilization of experience. Living in the present, in a series of advancing presents, someone had recognized the eternity of the single moment. As T. S. Eliot put it for his generation: "Time past and time future / What might have been and what has been / Point to one end, which is always present." The secret of Emerson, one of his biographers has suggested, "may be conveyed in one word, the superlative, even superhuman value which he found in the unit of experience."

The motive and result of perception, of observation, of science is, says Emerson, "the extension of man, on all sides, till his hands shall touch the stars, his eye see through the earth, his ears understand the language of the beast and bird, and the sense of the world," until "through his sympathies heaven and earth shall talk with him." Wisdom is finally discovered, not through partaking of other men's wisdom, but through daily experience in the fresh perception of elemental things. "Let us have," he said, "a robust, manly life; let us know what we know, for certain; let it be solid and seasonable and our own. A world in the hand is worth two in the bush. Let us have to do with real men and women, and not skipping ghosts."

For himself, said Emerson, he could do without "the learned lecture . . . and libraries, / Institutions and dictionaries"; when in their place he could listen to the sharp, direct speech of men in taverns,

> Which keeps the ground and never soars
> While Jake retorts and Reuben roars;
> Scoff of yeoman strong and stark,
> Goes like a bullet to its mark.

"There is a great deal of self-denial and manliness in poor and middle-class houses . . . that has not," he said, "got into literature . . . but that keeps the earth sweet." In another mood, he called himself

The Invariable Mark of Wisdom

a willow of the wilderness,
Loving the wind that bent me. All my hurts
My garden spade can heal. A woodland walk,
A guest for water-grapes, a mocking thrush,
A wild rose, a rock-loving columbine,
Salve my worst wounds.

Nature, the world about him, that which existed solely that he might perceive it, was, he said, "an endless combination and repetition of a very few laws. She hums the old well-known air through innumerable variations."

This insistence on the value to man of a present perception of the simple and elemental is central also to Emerson's conception of literature. "The writer," he said, "is secretary, who is to report the doings of the miraculous spirit of life." "Writing," he said again, "is the greatest of the arts, the subtilest, and of most miraculous effect." One does not come by it easily. "The laws of composition are as strict as those of sculpture and architecture," he reminds himself in his journal. "There is always one line that ought to be drawn, or one proportion that should be kept, and every other line or proportion is wrong. . . . So in writing there is always a right word, and every other is wrong. . . . The effect of a fanciful word misplaced, is like that of a horn of exquisite polish growing on a human head." Emerson agreed with Schlegel that "in good prose every word is underlined." He said of a poem that it is only successful when "there is not a single line—nor word but expresses something that is true." And truth resides in simplicity: "Melodious poets," he says in his essay on Swedenborg, "should be hoarse as street ballads when once the penetrating key-note of nature and spirit is sounded—the earth-beat, sea-beat, heart-beat which makes the tune to which the sun rolls, and the globule of blood, and the sap of trees."

There is no bard in all the choir,
Not Homer's self, the poet sure,
Wise Milton's odes of pensive pleasure,

Ralph Waldo Emerson

> Or Shakespeare, whom no mind can measure,
> Nor Collins' verse of tender pain,
> Nor Byron's clarion of disdain,
> Scott, the delight of generous boys,
> Or Wordsworth, Pan's recording voice,—
> Not one of these can put in verse,
> Or to his presence could rehearse
> The sights and voices ravishing
> The boy knew on the hills in spring,
> When pacing through the oaks he heard
> Sharp queries of sentry-bird,
> The heavy grouse's sudden whir,
> The rattle of the kingfisher.

He admires particularly the mature simplicity in the *Essais* of Montaigne: "I know not anywhere," he says, "the book that seems less written. It is the language of conversation transferred to a book. Cut the words, and they would bleed." Men who write like this trip in their speech no more than do the men in the tavern, Jake and Reuben, the blacksmith or teamster—theirs "is a shower of bullets. It is Cambridge men who correct themselves and begin again at every half sentence, and . . . pun and refine too much" instead of speaking without hesitation to the point like Montaigne. People who ape fashions grasp at "modish innovation, and the learned depart from the established forms of speech, in hope of finding or making" something superficially new; thinking to elevate themselves, they "forsake the vulgar, when the vulgar is right." Such intellectual pretension defeats itself. It does not communicate. It arrives at convictions, as H. L. Mencken once said, through manipulation of inherited prejudices. Its words, instead of hugging the ground, William Faulkner was to say, go up in the air like smoke.

Prominent among people of this class are the scholars, a studiously derivative people: "they are thin and pale, their feet are cold, their heads are hot, the night is without sleep, the day a fear of interruption,—pallor, squalor, hunger and egotism. If you come near them and see what conceits they entertain,—they are abstractionists, and spend their days and nights in dreaming some dream; in expecting the homage of society to some precious scheme, built on a truth, but destitute of proportion in its presentment." Their words are stale, their books unread, their names forgotten. They feed upon themselves oblivious of the living and lively world that surrounds them.

There is, however, "in every nation a style which never becomes obsolete." It is "to be sought," says Emerson in his brief essay on "Art and Criticism," "in the common intercourse of life, among those who speak only to be understood, without ambition of elegance." "Talent," he says elsewhere, "makes counterfeit ties; genius finds the real ones." This is the "costly charm of the ancient tragedy" of Aeschylus and Sophocles, he tells us in his essay on "History,"—"that the persons speak simply,—speak as persons who have great sense without knowing it, before the reflective habit has become the predominant habit of the mind. Our admiration of the antique," he says, "is not admiration of the old, but of the natural. Among the Greeks, perfect in their senses and in their health, . . . adults acted with the simplicity and grace of children."

That is the quality that Chaucer had, and Shakespeare, within whose plays circulated "the rude warm blood of living England" which "gave body . . . to his airy and majestic fancy." That is what Dante had, and Rabelais, Montaigne, and Bacon; and Luther also, who explained: "I preach coarsely; that giveth content to all." It is what Goethe lost when he constructed the second part of his *Faust,* not from "wild miraculous songs, but from elaborate forms to which he confided a retrospective philosophy. It is "the terrible gift of familiarity" shared by Swift, Defoe, and Carlyle, men who dare "speak with the vulgar," but "think with the wise." Even Plato relieved the exquisite refinement of his argument by introducing the low-born Socrates, who spices the dialogues "by his perverse talk, his gallipots, and cook, and trencher, and cart-wheels—and

Ralph Waldo Emerson

steadily kept up the coarseness to flavor a dish else too luscious."

This was more than an adaptation by Emerson of seventeenth-century doctrines of plain style, though he gloried in and found his greatest admirations in that century, in Herrick and Milton, and "golden voiced" Jeremy Taylor; it was more, as has been said, than a Yankee rephrasing of Wordsworth's concern with simple people whose essential nature is not crusted over by a veneer of civilization or sophistication. Simplicity was to be sought because only through simplicity might man pierce to the simple and elemental truths of nature.

Emerson recognized that it was more difficult to be simple than to be complex, to be a person of one piece rather than a kaleidoscope of other people's opinions. Words being the only means by which man can articulate his apprehension, desires, or sorrows, Emerson would therefore encourage use of the most simple and simply explicit words. "I deal in solemn truths," he said. "I have no ambition to startle you with sounding paradoxes." To make his point, he recommended "not only low style, but the lowest classifying words," words "which outvalue arguments; as upstart, dab, cockney, prig, granny, lubber, puppy, peacock." He advised short Saxon words: "The language of the street," he said, "is always strong. I envy the boys the force of the double negative (no shoes, no money, no nothing) . . . and I confess to some titillation of my ears from a rattling oath." He suggested that some men even "swear with genius."

After naturalness, the writer must strive for brevity, compression, what Emerson calls "the science of omitting." "The silences, pauses of an orator," he reminds us, "are as telling as his words. What the poet omits exalts every syllable that he writes." No word, as he had said, was to be used but the right word, and the shorter the better. He listed in his essay on "Art and Criticism" the kind of words which tempt young writers or immature thinkers, the multi-syllabic words or words worn threadbare by misuse. He

The Invariable Mark of Wisdom

pointed again to words as symbols, presenting images of fact: "Everything," he reminds us once more, "has two handles." In his essay on Montaigne he explains that "every fact is related on the one side to sensation, and on the other to morals. The game of thought is, on the appearance of one of these sides, to find the other: given the upper, to find the underside. Nothing so thin but has these two faces, and when the observer has seen the obverse, he turns it over to see the reverse. Life is a pitching of pennies,—heads or tails. We never tire of the game because there is still a slight shudder of astonishment at the exhibition of the other face, at the contrast of the two faces."

In his own quest for compression, Emerson crackles with epigrams. He bombards with buckshot and peppers with cannonballs. He is richly assertive, insistently provocative. Suggestion is folded upon suggestion, each one intimating something implicit in the other, each one itself a suggestion of truth, but each one—perhaps because of imperfection in Emerson, perhaps because of imperfection in the reader— seeming to contradict or amend the other. We may become impatient with him because he builds on no logical structure, forgetting that he has told us that logic is a shortcut that does not lead inevitably toward truth. John Dewey, who described Emerson as "the one citizen of the New World fit to have his name uttered in the same breath with that of Plato," suggested that "even if Emerson has no system, none the less he is the prophet and herald of any system which democracy may henceforth construct and hold by." And Dewey defends Emerson's kind of logic, which is not unlike that which has developed in our own relativistic twentieth century, by saying: "I am not acquainted with any writer, no matter how assured his position in treatises on the history of philosophy, whose movement of thought is more compact and unified." And he quoted Emerson, who had explained: "Logic is the procession or unfolding of the intuition; but its virtue is as silent method; that moment it

Ralph Waldo Emerson

would appear as propositions and have separate value, it is worthless." The insight felt, the word spoken, the revelation articulated, then it moves toward the past to become part of a pattern. Man's eternal quest is to move beyond pattern, remaining perceptively in the present, avoiding what would shackle him.

The record of that quest is in literature. "The art of writing," Emerson says, "is the highest of those permitted to man as drawing directly from the soul, and the means or materials it uses are also of the soul. It brings man into alliance with what is great and eternal. It discloses to him the variety and splendor of his resources. And there is much in literature that draws us with a sublime charm—the superincumbent necessity by which each writer, an infirm, capricious, fragmentary soul, is made to utter his part in the chorus of humanity, is enriched by thoughts which flow from all past minds, shares the hope of all existing minds; so that whilst the world is made of youthful, helpless children of a day, literature resounds with the music of united vast ideas of affirmation and moral truth."

For all the argument or reservations set forth against him—that he derives from Wordsworth, feeds on Coleridge, admires Scott—Emerson himself refuses the label of romantic. Romantic art to him is the haphazard product of caprice; it is irresponsible; it contains no health, no strength, no effective solace or insight. The kind of art that Emerson approved was healthy, directed by necessity, inevitable, organic. Its concern is with beauty that is natural harmony, not beauty that is manipulated to form.

"We ascribe beauty," he explains, "to that which is simple, which has no superfluous parts; which exactly answers its end. . . . Beyond their sensuous delight, the forms and colors of nature have a new charm for us in our perception that not one ornament was added for ornament, but each is a sign of some better health or more excellent action. The tree in autumn is ornamented, not for sake of

ornamentation, but that it may renew itself. Yet it is nonetheless beautiful. Nature seen clearly in proportion is all
beautiful": "The cat or the deer cannot walk inelegantly."
Beauty is simple: "This is the charm of running water, sea
waves, the flight of birds and the locomotion of animals."
It is useful: "The cell of the bee is built at that angle which
gives the most strength with the least wax; the bone or
quill of the bird gives the most . . . strength with the least
weight." Beauty, as we have already heard Emerson say,
is only beauty when it is inevitable, functional, utilitarian.
"It is the purgation of superficialities," said Michelangelo,
and Emerson seconds him by explaining, "In rhetoric, this
art of omission is the chief secret of power. . . . it is part of
high culture to say the greatest matter in the simplest way."

"Talent cannot make a writer," says Emerson as he dis-
cusses what he considered the ultimate failure of Goethe.
"There must be a man behind the book, a personality which
by birth and quality is pledged to the doctrines there set
forth, and which exists to see and state the things so, and
not otherwise." The poet is "no odd fellow who describes
strange and impossible situations," but is a "universal man
who pens a confession for one and all to see." He creates
no fables, only uncovers universal verities. He tries the
virtue of sincerity, for a "dilettantism in nature is barren
and unworthy. A fop of the fields is no better than his
brother of Broadway." Emerson plays many changes on
this, a favorite theme: "He who knows the most; he who
knows what sweets and virtues are in the ground, the waters,
the plants, the heavens, and how to come to these enchantments—is the rich and royal man. Only insofar as the
masters of the world have called in nature to their aid, can
they reach the height of magnificence."

How are we, who are not poets but only critical or ap-
preciative readers, to appraise the poet's product? What
measure may we place against it? How estimate its worth?
Emerson's answer is direct. "A man of genius or a work of
love or beauty," he says, "will not come to order, can't be

compounded by the best rules, but is always a new and incalculable result." The play is not to be considered in relation to *Hamlet*, but in relation to itself. The poet is not a new Milton, but a new man. Every work of art, organically a unit, creates its own pattern. Every poet discovers his own insight, reaches for his own idiom, creates his own manner of formulation. He is never capricious, nor is his art capricious, for its regulation is from within. "Don't rattle your rules in our ears," warns Emerson; "we must behave as we can. Criticism is an art when it does not stop at the words of the poet, but looks at the order of his thoughts and the essential quality of his mind. Then the critic is poet."

VI

The All-Knowing Spirit

HOWEVER MUCH he speaks of poetry and art, sincerity and simplicity, the cornerstone of Emerson's thought is sturdily laid on religious ground inherited from his ancestors. Whatever temples he erected upon it to beauty or duty, to character and moral sense, his basis throughout is religious. Though called atheist by some who resented his unwillingness to accept their opinions, Emerson is never atheist. The light that penetrates the darkness of the material world is a light that comes from God, who "is the eternal, extempore, creative power, sustaining and superintending the universe which he has designed, not for his own glory, but for the benefit of mankind." God is the all-knowing spirit, elusive, but whose truth was eternal. "I count it," said Emerson, "the great object of my life to explore nature of God."

This God of creation and illumination was not the absentee landlord God of the eighteenth-century rationalist. He was not the God who put the world together in the perfect harmony of a vast and smoothly running machine, who set the machine in motion and then withdrew from the world which ran its course according to the mechanical principles he had devised. Emerson's God was a living God, as active today as ever before, continually creating, and available anew to people of every generation, who are not only dependent on him for their origin, but for what they had become or might have become had they sought him more often. He offered to each opportunities for fresh revelation of his divine intention. Nature was a gateway to those revelations, and nature to Emerson was everything that was not spirit; not only trees and flowers, mountains and lakes, sunrise and sunset, and starlit or moonlit nights, but his own body also with all of its sensory apparatus. Emerson has been called a pantheist, but he was not. God was not nature. God was not present in all nature. Nature only provided symbols, hints, analogues of the God who, however named, existed within and above all people—the Over-Soul, the all-knowing spirit. Without his continuing availability there could be no intelligence, only learning; no conscience, only custom; no revelation, only acceptance of outworn creed.

Too many men "make their religion an historical religion," Emerson said. "They see God in Judea and in Egypt, in Moses and in Jesus, but not around them. We want a living religion. As the faith was alive in the hearts of Abraham and Paul, so I would have it in mine. I want a religion not recorded in a book but flowing from all things." Emerson had little formal theology. Popular religious liberalism as expounded by William Ellery Channing, at whose church the Emersons were communicants after the Reverend William Emerson's death in 1811, the austere religious orthodoxy of his Aunt Mary Moody Emerson, his own preparation for the ministry, all had a share in the forming of his convictions.

But these convictions seem to have been formed more by what he read in the poets than in the theologians. He was what was popularly known in his time a "Channing Unitarian," one who broke away from Calvinism because of its austere requirements. But he was led even beyond that contemporary Unitarianism by his readings in Wordsworth and Coleridge, Goethe and Schleiermacher until finally there was formed within him a Promethean ambition to purify not only the old Calvinistic faith, but also the new liberal Unitarian faith, to keep it also from slipping into placid acceptance instead of searching and discovering new intimations of divinity. He was thus what in the seventeenth

The All-Knowing Spirit

century would have been called a Puritan, a man who would purify, remove inherited dross from religion. Religion should not be bound by dogma, subject to ancient revelation. It must remain open to the new revelation which each new day could bring.

The poet, both see-er and sayer, speaks from transcendental reason which reaches beyond sensory perception to recognize the inevitable and eternal correspondence of nature and spirit. He speaks not from Understanding, which is concerned with the expedient, the day-by-day customary concerns which look to history, economics, institutions, or the opinions of contemporaries for guidance. Devout in attendance on the God within, he speaks what had not been spoken before. Every fact, every observation contains for him an explanatory revelation of truth which is eternal. Such insight is available to all persons not held earthbound, recognizing only surfaces. But words are needed if truth is to be told. The poet-sayer who speaks in words before unspoken, speaks as the true, though inevitably diminished, voice of God, opening gateways which reveal, even fleetingly, the power, the grace, the kindly admonitions of the God within who is the all-knowing spirit. The beauties thus revealed approximate holiness.

For all its posture of revolt this was, however, but fine old wine in an attractive new bottle, a repetition in expanded terms of many certainties expressed by Puritan colonials of the seventeenth century like Thomas Shepard and Thomas Hooker, and in the eighteenth century by Jonathan Edwards. The confident restrictions that had once upheld protestant faith, and that in more modern times proudly and publicly had acknowledged that all men were created equal, were stripped of inherited limitation. Old beliefs were reaffirmed, but in new idioms—of transcendental idealism, of Platonism in its variety of forms, of Swedenborg, Coleridge, and the *Bhagavad-gita*, all revealed in the eclectic language of Emerson's "Over-Soul," his "Brahma," his heady essay on "Self-Reliance," and his first essay on *Nature*.

The nineteenth-century descendants of the Puritans to whom Emerson spoke declined adherence to the notion that the visible fabric of nature presented only to a God-elected few the shadowed images of divine truths, like the inexpressible immensity, the power and the redeeming grace of God. Emerson gave calm assurance that this ecstasy of insight was available to all. When "currents of the Universal Being circulate through me," he said, "I am part or parcel with God." The universal essence which he named the Over-Soul and which embraced as one all beauty, love, wisdom, and power, was revealed through nature, accessible to every perceptive person. Salvation was available to all. Those who would claim their inheritance were indeed children of God whose essence each contained and of whom nature was both alphabet and index.

Perception was the secret—perception, as Henry James would explain, at the peak of passion. But perception in quiethood also. Take all my senses, Emerson once said, but save me my eyes. To see beneath appearance, and, in seeing, discovering belief—was not that in truth true religion?

Emerson, a unitarian, was in revolt against the rationalistic materialism of the Boston Unitarianism in which he had been reared. Perhaps it was because Emerson had been a poor boy in a wealthy, traditional, self-satisfied, and self-assured society that the Unitarianism of William Ellery Channing seemed to him hardly more than a cautious compromise. A sturdy structure, perhaps, but one resting on a crumbling foundation. It was increasingly the religion of the well-to-do, respectable middle class of Boston and Cambridge, of sensible men of common sense, successful in things of the world. Once itself the religion of revolt, it was becoming the constituted creed of those who would conform. Unitarianism was practical—there were no mysteries in it;

it explained miracles; it managed to establish Jesus and
Paul as men of persuasion, successful in disseminating important precepts. It was becoming the religion of men proud
of strength and workaday prosperity, of men who saw
clearly through illusion, who had no truck with any miracles
but those of their own making. Like Hawthorne's watch-
maker, they could understand what they could touch, and
nothing else. To them conception in any but the usual manner was clearly a scientific impossibility; miracles were
legerdemain or old wives' tales. The progressive new religion of New England had become the servant of men more
at ease in the counting house or at champagne and oyster
suppers than at the table of the Lord. It was the religion
of men of understanding, with all mystery gone. Unitarianism became factual, unimaginative, pallid, unexciting—as
unsatisfying to Emerson as it was to be to Melville or to
Emily Dickinson who sought mystical manifestations of
spiritual grace, one in roving in fact and imagination through
the world, the other quietly at home in Amherst.

"The doctrine of inspiration is lost," Emerson complained;
"the base doctrine of the majority of voices usurps the
place of the doctrine of the soul. Miracles, prophecy, poetry,
the ideal life, the holy life, exist as ancient history merely;
they are not in the belief, nor in the aspiration of society;
but, when suggested, seem ridiculous. Life is comic or pitiful
as soon as the high ends of being fade out of sight, and man
becomes near-sighted, and can only attend to what addresses
the senses." And life, to one who is perceptive, is not comic
nor pitiful, not even tragic; it is a pageant planned by God
within which may be discovered suggestions of mystery
infinitely more compelling than life which is only the
opposite of death. Life must continue to excite and inspire,
or man dies before his time.

Most Americans, Emerson might have said, die at thirty,
buried in the mire of established opinion. They are com-
placent conformers for more than half of their lives, until

finally and fearfully committed to the grave, without ever having known the miracles daily repeated through the living spirit of God ever actively present. To vitalize religion, dogmas that were remnants of the past must be cast aside. Like their Calvinist ancestors, Emerson and his kind sought for muted murmurings of the holy spirit within and for symbolic representations of that spirit in nature. The restraining hand of traditional theology withdrawn, they identified their intuition as the voice of God, a dangerous practice indeed unless kept under the kinds of control on which Emerson insisted, for, as he consistently warned, illness, temperament, even vagaries of weather might distort a person's interpretations of the voice within. But the voice was there, available, waiting to be heard. Listening to it, a person might become an immediate identifier of the true, the beautiful, and the good.

Emerson's mission was to spiritualize Unitarianism, to refreshen and revitalize the new religion by finding in it some of the power of ecstasy which had been within the old. His attitude toward Jesus was not remarkably different from that of other religious liberals of his day. Jesus to him was the reincarnation of the preexistent Logos, or Word: the "Word made flesh." He is, Emerson says in his Journal, "the minister of pure Reason." He belonged, he explained in the Divinity School Address, "to the true race of prophets. He saw with open eye the mystery of the soul. Drawn by its severe harmony, ravished with its beauty, he lived in it, and had his being there. Alone in all history he estimated the greatness of man. He saw that God incarnates himself in man, and ever more goes forth anew to take possession of his World. He said, . . . 'I am divine. Through me God acts, through me, speaks.' " Potentially all persons share with Jesus the same indwelling spirit. Each is a son of God.

Jesus, then, is a man; but he is also divine in the sense that he was able to interpret revelations of the divinity within himself—the God within. In an early sermon, entitled "Trust Yourself," Emerson proclaims the "great calamity under which all men are contending after all the preaching of Christianity in their distrust of themselves. They do not know, because they have not tried, the spiritual force that belongs to them." This Jesus did know. He recognized the Word, the truth within himself. And this all men can know. Here again is the center of Emerson's gospel— its religious center. If each man will trust himself and recognize the avenue toward truth within himself, he also may know God, and he can reincarnate—give body, substance, form to the Word, even as Jesus did.

Looking about him in the early 1830s, Emerson saw a "great tendency to uniformity of action and conversation among men." It stunted man, who sat among his conventions, a god in ruins, fallen because he would not recognize the divinity within him, because he would not become a son of God. He was imitative; he was a secondary man; he lacked confidence; he lacked trust; he was atheist because he failed to allow God to speak. Yet, said Emerson, "Let him fully trust his own share of God's goodness, that if used to the uppermost, it will lead him unto a perfection which has no type yet in the universe, save only in the Divine Mind."

This was heady and intoxicating doctrine, to which many in nineteenth-century America joyously responded. It fit the buoyant spirit of the times. It lent itself to imitation as much as to parody. A great new country was expanding westward and man expanded with it. There seemed no limits to the development of either. There is divinity which is truth and rightness in every man, just as there had been divinity in Jesus.

Jesus spoke with authority and not as one of the Scribes —he spoke, that is, as a result of revelation, not tradition. He spoke with authority, says Emerson, because "he taught truth, and the supreme kind of truth (that which relates to man's moral nature) with greater fidelity and distinctive-

ness than any other; because he taught more truth, . . .
more truly; because he did not, as other teachers, drop here
and there a good hint, a valuable fragment, but plainly
announced the leading principles by which whilst the soul
exists, it must be governed; because, speaking on his own
convictions, he expressed with unexampled force, the great
laws to which the human understanding must always
bow. . . . He spoke of God in a new tongue, not as philosophers had done, as an intellectual principle, . . . but in
terms of earnest affection as being best understood by us
as the Father of the human soul, the grand object of all
thought, and that the end of life was a preparation of the
soul to approach him by likeness of character." Thus
Emerson spoke in an early sermon in which he attempted
to define "The Authority of Jesus," setting forth in his
thirties an attitude that he would spend much of his life
in explaining, circling outward around it to make it more
clear.

Jesus, even more than Plato, Shakespeare, or Swedenborg,
was Emerson's great hero, the man who in all history came
closest to the human ideal, who in his human life most fully
incarnated the truth of God. He represented the highest
virtues of man as set forth by the nineteenth-century romantic, transcendental idea. Stripped of the convention of
divinity, revealed as man—like, though better than, other
men—he was not an object of worship but of emulation.
Man could attempt to be like Jesus, who was man, without
committing the heresy of attempting to be God. Emerson
thus, I think, escapes the charge which Allen Tate makes
against Edgar Allan Poe—the charge of reaching that kind
of psychic imbalance which permits man to imagine himself
not an incarnation but the Word itself.

It is probably true that almost every man creates his
ideal in his own image. And Emerson, who would be simple,
perceptive, and direct, found these qualities in Jesus. "He

The All-Knowing Spirit

was not learned. He does not," says Emerson, "appear to have any better education than a Jewish peasant. . . . He was not a subtle reasoner. . . . He proved nothing by argument. He simply asserts, on the ground of his divine commission. Every one of his declarations is a naked appeal to every man's consciousness." He spoke, that is, as a prophet speaks. He spoke as Emerson spoke. He spoke also as William Faulkner spoke when, in accepting the Nobel Prize, he spoke of humility and love and a recognition by man of man's place in the universe as that which alone can redeem man. It is, said Emerson 100 years before Faulkner —but some nineteen hundred years after Jesus—"humility, love, self-denial," these three which supply the means by which man can approach the human greatness of Jesus. These, said Emerson, are "the true glories of man. To have them was to have life." He says much the same thing in "The Over-Soul": "Those who are capable of humility, of justice, of love, of aspiration, stand already on a platform that commands the sciences and arts, speech and poetry, action and grace."

Of Jesus, he explains further: "He is our Saviour and Redeemer not because oil was poured on his head, nor because he descended by his mother of the line of David, nor because prophets predicted him or miracles attended him nor for all of these reasons, but because he declared for the first time truly and intelligibly those truths on which the welfare of the human soul depends: because he declared them not as formal propositions but in a full apprehension of their commanding importance, he lived by them." So must all men who would redeem their manhood. "Jesus is loved and followed in proportion not as men cower and name and obey the letter of his commands in a slavish spirit, but as they generously embark in the same cause by word and act; open the elementary truths he gave them; carry it out to further conclusions; and each to be to their own age as nearly as they can the excellent benefactor which

Ralph Waldo Emerson

he has been to so many ages and nations." We also, he said in his essay on Goethe, "must write Bibles, to unite again [for our time] the heavens and the earthly world."

That was what Emerson would do, and that is what made him in everything but the formal sense one of the most truly religious men of his time. What was shocking in his Divinity School Address at Harvard was that he said these things plainly: first, that the person and not the spirit of Jesus had become the object of veneration among his contemporaries, and, second, that men in nineteenth-century America regarded God as if he were dead, so that "on Sundays it seems almost wicked to go to church," so hollow and withered and worn its creeds and observances. "The doctrine of inspiration is lost; the base doctrine of the majority of voices usurps the place of the doctrine of the soul. Miracles, prophecy, poetry, the ideal life, the holy life, exist as ancient history merely." Life is not regal, but "comic or pitiful, as soon as the high ends fade out of sight, and man becomes near-sighted, and can only attend to what addresses the senses."

It seemed to Emerson that there had been three great eras in the religion of the western world. In the first, the Greeks had deified nature, spiritualizing the material world by providing a hierarchy of gods and goddesses, each with special functions or responsibilities. In the second, the Christian era, emphasis was on redemption; nature and what came naturally was the domain of evil presided over by Satan. Heaven rose above nature. But, in the third, the post-Christian era, people "retrace their steps and rally again on Nature," neither to deify nor diabolize it, but to discover in it through observation, science, and imagination the unfolding of new truths hitherto unforetold. Not a scientist himself, Emerson recognized science as an instrument of revelation, and the need, he said, "was never greater of a new revelation than now."

Emerson devoted his life to seeking that revelation,

The All-Knowing Spirit

exercising "the spirit of prophecy which is innate in every man." His words had purpose beyond the conventions of what is often too casually called literature. Literature was likely to be only a painted show, a deception, a skillful manipulation of superficial reactions, tempting the emotions to insufficient or ignoble purposes. It skimmed prettily over the surface. It lulled and numbed rather than reaching with invigorating power toward essentials. "The great distinction," he said, "between teachers sacred or literary—between poets like Herbert, and poets like Pope,—between philosophers like Spinoza, Kant, and Coleridge, and philosophers like Locke, Paley, Mackintosh and Stewart, who are reckoned accomplished talkers, and here and there a fervent mystic, prophesying half insane under the infinitude of his thought,—is that one class speak from *within,* or from experience, as parties and possessors of the fact; and the other class from *without,* as spectators merely, or perhaps as acquainted with the fact on the evidence of third persons. It is no use to preach to me from without. I can do that too easily myself. Jesus speaks always from within, and in a degree that transcends all others. In that is the miracle." That is the manner in which Emerson would speak.

"Among the multitude of scholars and authors," he said, "we feel no allowing presence; we are sensible of a knack and skill rather than of inspiration; . . . their talent is some exaggerated faculty, some overgrown member, so their strength is a disease" and their "intellectual gifts do not make the impression of virtue, but almost of vice; and we feel that a man's talents stand in the way of his advancement in truth." So much for literature, so much for talent. "But genius is religious. . . . There is in all poets a wisdom of humanity which is superior to any talents they exercise. The author, the wit, the partisan, the fine gentleman, does not take the place of the man. Humanity shines in Chaucer, in Spenser, in Shakespeare, in Milton. They are content with truth. . . . Converse with a mind that is grandly simple, and literature looks like word-catching. The simplest utterances are worthiest to be written."

Emerson then did not think of himself as a man of letters in the usual sense. He was a teacher, a seer, a prophet, with aspiration to relive the kind of perceptive experience which made Jesus seer and prophet. "There are," he explained, "all degrees of proficiency in knowledge of the world. . . . One class live to the utility of the symbol, esteeming health and wealth a final good. Another class live above this mark to the beauty of the symbol, as the poet and artist and the naturalist and man of science. A third class live above the beauty of the symbol to the beauty of the thing signified; these are the wise men. The first class have common sense; the second, taste, and the third spiritual perception." And it is to this third class that Emerson would belong.

He counts himself out as a man of letters. He is not poet because he would be more than poet. He would be perceiver and translator of the mysteries of the universe; his the new revelation, rephrasing in the light of what man knows today the simple truths of the Sermon on the Mount. His ambition was incredible, but his achievement immense. Emerson epitomizes much of what was best thought and said in his century. He was gladly a supreme egoist. His head was often in the clouds. He was leader of what has been called the party of hope, an advocate of the bootstrap theory of progress.

Those who consider themselves more sophisticated than he may find his comprehensive acceptance more irritating than helpful, his thought an episode from a vanished past. Yet Emerson is something more than an historical artifact, to be studied as an arch representative of the ultimate in star-reaching theory. He is more than just an influence on Thoreau and Whitman, Emily Dickinson, Robert Frost, and many another. For all his denial of simply literary intention he remains one of the truly representative men of American literature. He moves within a tradition of which for his time he was principal spokesman, and which, despite worldly opposition, continues into ours.

For "it is not true," Stephen Whicher has said, "that he has nothing to say to us. Emerson believed in the dignity of human life more unreservedly, almost, than any one who has ever written. Man possesses, he felt, an unlimited capacity for spiritual growth and is surrounded by influences that perpetually call on him for the best he has of insight and greatness and virtue and love. We think more meanly now, no doubt more truly, of ourselves and our world. But as long as we retain any self-respect, something in us must answer—whatever the second thoughts—to the faith in man that invigorates every page of [his] volumes. To reject Emerson utterly is to reject mankind."

The Conduct of Life

VII

The Real Price of Labor

NATURE IS BOTH servant to man and a bountiful provider. It offers gifts that he at his peril refuses. It offers him sustenance, as he feeds on its bounty. A prudent man depends on nature to keep his larder full, his woodpile well stacked, his clothing tight or light as seasons change. An inventive man will use his knowledge of nature to devise a better mousetrap or capture steam within an engine, and the world will flock to his door, bringing wealth, leisure, ease. This ameliorating legacy of nature is ancient and universal, shared with man by tree and plant, by ant, squirrel, beaver, and woodchuck, each prudently utilizing nature's abundant resources to its own advantage. Though not nature's greatest gift, it is primary, for without it others could not exist. People must prudently discipline themselves alike to nature's demands and to its rewards in wealth and well-being.

Nature is not only a generous giver to those who will accept her bounty. She is also a stern disciplinarian to those who through sloth or ignorance fail to take advantage of her offerings. She can freeze, she can drown, she can impoverish. Men must work to eat; they must eat to prosper; they must prosper if they will avail themselves of their right share of nature's offerings. "Wealth," Emerson was to say, "begins in a tight roof that keeps the wind and rain out; in a good pump that yields you plenty of fresh water; in two suits of clothes, so to change your dress when you are wet; in dry sticks to burn, and three meals; in a horse or locomotive to cross the land, in a boat to cross the sea; in

111

Ralph Waldo Emerson

tools to work with, in books to read." But money, he said, "represents the prose of life." In his early essay on "Compensation," he had assured readers, "The real price of labor is knowledge and virtue, whereof wealth and credit are signs."

Emerson shared with his time the optimistic certainty that men might through strenuous endeavor make each generation better and more advanced than the generation before. He believed in the idea of progress, and he knew that nowhere was progress more immediately possible than in the expanding United States. He shared with his countrymen an economic optimism based on the belief that the resources of America were inexhaustible, that America was in truth the land of opportunity. "The bountiful continent of ours," he called it. "We cannot look on the freedom of this country . . . without a presentiment that here shall laws and institutions exist on some scale of proportion to the majesty of nature." Here, amid limitless opportunities, great men might rise. Thus civilization advances. "The world is all gates," he said, "all opportunities."

Wealth meant well-being. Emerson envied his young friend Thoreau's practical conquest of nature, taking from it only what was needed for simplest existence. He sympathized with his friend Bronson Alcott, so immune to consideration of practicalities that his family often suffered want. They and people like them who put aside things of the world for things of the spirit were people of lofty aims, reminding him of his aunt Mary Moody Emerson's telling him in his youth that her "grandfather prayed every night that none of his descendants might be rich." It was she who had taught him that it was better to do without than to gain "at too great a cost," a statement which Thoreau, a more able and consistent economist, improved by explaining that the cost of anything is the amount of life which must be exchanged for it. Some of the greatest men of all time had cared little for money. Emerson often thought of

The Real Price of Labor

Socrates and Jesus and St. Paul with admiration, perhaps envy.

He never forgot what he had so confidently expressed in his essay on "Intellect," that "God offers to each mind its choice between truth and repose. Take what you please— you can never have both. Between these, as a pendulum, man oscillates. He in whom love of freedom predominates will accept the first creed, the first philosophy, the first political party he meets,—most likely his father's. He gets rest, commodity and reputation; but he shuts the door to truth. He in whom love of truth predominates will keep himself aloof from all moorings, and afloat. He will abstain from dogmatism, and recognize all opposite negations between which as walls, his being is swung. He submits to the inconvenience of suspense and imperfect opinion, but he is a candidate for truth, as the other is not, and represents the highest law of his being."

But Emerson had also an inherited sense of responsibility for such things as the care and comfort of family. He had learned the necessity of careful economy in protecting his never quite robust health. He knew from his own experience that having money was more pleasant than being without it. In his boyhood, he had known the clutching grasp of poverty: "debt, grinding debt, whose face the widow, the orphan, and the son of genius fear and hate . . . is a preceptor," he wrote, "whose lessons cannot be forgotten." Thrift and industry were familiar Yankee virtues that Emerson had learned early.

One of nature's great services was that it taught a person to discipline himself, to learn foresight, frugality, willpower. Puritan New England had been noted for its double concern with cash and conscience. Competence and carefulness were commendable virtues: "Every man's wealth," Emerson believed, "is an index to his merit." Prudent men who read nature rightly became men of property. Indolent men remained poor, pernicious in their demands and influence. In his essay on "Nominalist and Realist" in 1846, he explained, "Property keeps the accounts of the world, and is always moral. The property is to be found where the labor, wisdom, and the virtue have been in nations, in classes, and . . . the individual."

Nature was generous in its offerings. It provided sensory pleasures, opportunities for the enjoyment of what struck the eye or ear as beautiful; it provided opportunity for the utilization of its bounteous resources, in plowing, planting, providing shelter and sustenance, and allowed the person who understood even the simplest of her laws to devise formulas or machines which properly managed could bring wealth and power: "the good man will be the wise man," Emerson said in his essay on "Prudence." He resented the observation of a clergyman acquaintance that "houses and lands, offices, wine, horses, dress, luxury, are had by unprincipled men, whilst saints are poor and despised." So sweeping a generality did not withstand the evidence of experience. "All the virtues," he said, "range themselves on the side of prudence, or the art of receiving a present well-being." In his essay on "Nature" he said, "He who knows the most; he who knows what sweets and virtues are in the ground, the waters, the plants, the heavens, and how to come on these enchantments,—is the rich and royal man."

In addressing the Mechanics' Apprentices' Library Association of Boston in 1841 he urged each member of his young audience to stand on his own feet, doing his own thing with whatever talent had been allowed him. He spoke then of the sins of trade, "grown selfish to the borders of theft" and "the trail of the serpent reaches into all the lucrative professions of man." He urged them to put themselves "into primary relations with the soil and nature," each selecting employment according to his own unique skill, reminding them that even manual labor "is the study of the external world." The "man who supplies his own want, who builds a raft or a boat to go a-fishing, finds it easy to caulk it, or put in the thole pin, or mend the rudder," for he is rich in understanding the resources of nature. "Why must he have horses, fine garments, handsome apartments, access to public houses and places of amusement? Only for want of thought," for lack of reliance on a right relation to nature. True riches are not inherited. Every generation must create its own. "What is man for but to be a Reformer, a Re-maker of what man has made, a renouncer of lies, a restorer of truth and good, imitating that great Nature which embosoms us all." Richness does not "rely on the power of the dollar," but on the industrious rectitude of the individual. Wealth results from the proper management of things of the world, beyond which and through which is access to the god within. "The opening of the spiritual senses disposes men," he told them, "to cast all things behind in the insatiable thirst for divine communication."

If the world were to improve and people become more wise, nature's secrets must be more completely understood. Increased knowledge and application of her laws could bring riches to the person who interpreted them correctly. The opportunity was abundantly there. Nature's bounty was measureless. The knowledgeable, the perceptive, the imaginative man would utilize it, building railroads, delving for oil, dredging canals for the benefit of his fellows and his own personal gain.

A common criticism of Emerson has been that as he grew older and more comfortably supplied with easements that money supplied his attitude toward wealth changed. When he is read casually, sentences quoted out of context, he may be made to seem the patron saint of the Gilded Age, providing texts for the industrial barons of the late nineteenth century. Read partially, he tempted H. L. Mencken to exclaim, "It is one of the mysteries of American life that Rotary has never discovered Emerson. His so-called philosophy, even more than that of Elbert Hubbard, seems to be made precisely for the luncheon-table idealists." The truth is that, knowing it or not, the Rotary Clubs in this country and abroad have assimilated some of Emerson's best aspiring, more practical thought. And not only the Rotary Clubs, but other modern institutions, often taking from Emerson that part which best pleased their aspirations. One that comes to mind is the Christian Science of Mary Baker Eddy; another is the method of interpreting the world and man's place in it called Personalism. One Quaker friend has admitted that when he feels called to speak out in meeting, he simply quotes or paraphrases something which Emerson had said. For Emerson, when read in part, can seem to be all things to almost all people, but read whole a remarkable consistency becomes apparent: an insistence from the beginning on the responsibility of the individual for self sufficiency, "the infinitude of the private man."

Emerson's attitude toward wealth did not change, except that as the nineteenth century advanced he used the word as a convenient metaphor adapted to the spirit of the time. As the new nation developed, stretching tentacles westward, he spoke of wealth more explicitly and more at length, expanding with more attentive precision attitudes which he had expressed with less emphasis before. The first essay in his first volume of *Essays,* published in 1841 when he was thirty-eight, explained: "We sympathize . . . in the prosperities of great men. . . . We honor the rich because they have eternally the freedom, power, and grace which we feel to be proper to man, proper to us." In his second volume five years later, speaking of "Nature," he marvels at how the face of the world has changed since the time of Noah: "The private poor man hath cities, ships, canals, bridges built for him." Wealth, he said then, "was good as it appeased the animal cravings, cured the smokey chimney, silenced the creaking door, brought friends together in a warm, quiet room."

What happened was that Emerson did not remain static,

The Real Price of Labor

chained to what has sometimes been made to seem a foolish consistency. He moved with the movement of his time when men of the middle class were rising to power. Railways and highways were beginning to criss-cross the face of the nation; instant communication with Europe was promised by the laying of the transatlantic cable; steam instead of sail conquered the oceans. The sewing machine eased the labor of the housewife. Giant industrial looms replaced the domestic spinning wheel. Bullion from the West was hurried eastward by rail. Urbanization was creating a new life-style. These could be powerful instruments for the betterment of man, and Emerson saw in them the potential for great good. Ecologists today may well shudder at his confident assurance, " 'Tis fit to see the forests fall / The steep be graded." But he was responding to the spirit of his expansive time, not ours, when nature, exhausted, gives warning that its bounty has not been wisely used.

There is nothing ambivalent about Emerson's attitude toward wealth, except that on this subject, as on almost all others, he recognized two sides to every aspect of man's relation to the world: that this was true, but that also true; that appearance often belied fact; that nature could give and nature take away. He never departed from assurance that reconciliation was only possible in those rare moments when a person could or would listen to the murmured precepts of the god within. In his "Ode to W. H. Channing," he said:

> There are laws discrete,
> Not reconciled,—
> Law for man and law for thing;
> The last builds town and fleet,
> But it runs wild,
> And doth the man unking.
> . . . .
> Let man serve law for man.

Ralph Waldo Emerson

He had never known, he said, a man as rich as he ought to be, if he used his every talent to wring from nature its bounty: "Dull people think it Fortune that makes one rich and another poor," but they are wrong, for the secret of wealth is foresight, prudence, discipline, "a balance or adjustment between what is agreeable to-day and the forecast of what will be valuable tomorrow."

He was pleased with what the industrial revolution had done to democratize England, where, though a "sporting duke may fancy that the state depends on the House of Lords, . . . the engineer sees that every stroke of the steam-piston gives value to the duke's land, fills it with tenants; doubles, quadruples, centuples the duke's capital, drawing the nobility into competition as stockholders in the mine, the canal, the railway." It was "the main fact of modern history," this workingman's creation of wealth: "The counting room maxims liberally expanded are laws of the Universe." Wealth earned through the application of these laws is different from wealth inherited. The heir becomes a drone, living expensively on legacies from the past. Only the producing man provides rightful well-being.

"For he is the rich man in whom the people are rich," Emerson said in his essay on "Wealth" in 1860, "and he is the poor man in whom the people are poor." Riches can build churches, endow universities, provide parks, support hospitals. "To be rich is to have a ticket of admission to the masterworks and chief men of every race. It is to have the sea by voyaging; to visit the mountains, Niagara, the Nile, the desert, Rome, Paris, Constantinople; to see the galleries, libraries, arsensals, manufacturers." In truth, the "world is his who has the money to go over it." Man was born to be rich: "Nature arms each man with some faculty which enables him to do easily some feat impossible to any other, and thus makes him necessary to society." To men of sense, wealth is "the assimilation of nature to themselves,

118

the converting of the saps and juices of the planet to the incarnation and nutriment of their design."

Wealth bred culture, appreciation of necessary and comfortable and ennobling things of the world. But wealth as he saw it increase in his burgeoning new country seemed often also to be self-defeating, feeding on itself. "The lesson of these days," he confided to his journal, "is the vulgarity of wealth. . . . Wealth will vote for rum, will vote for tyranny, will vote for slavery, will vote against the ballot, will vote against international copyright, will vote against schools, colleges, or any high direction of public money." He spoke bitterly of "the invincible depravity of the virtuous classes." Individualism was warped by industrialism: "The machine unmakes the man. . . . The weaver becomes a web, the machinist a machine."

Great men had wrung tremendous wealth from nature, but nature had its revenge as people became littler in struggles to maintain what in former strength other people had devised. The new industrial society threatened to consume the individual. As frontiers began to close, there was room only for men who would haggle and pinch to retain at any cost the power of wealth. Capitalism, born of the exploits of great men, spawned only little men, lost in a morass of mediocrity and conformity. Wealth itself became an institution; the age became retrospective.

Napoleon seemed to Emerson "the incarnate democrat," who had "in transcendent degree the qualities and powers of common men." Unembarrassed "by scruples; compact, instant, selfish, prudent, and of a perception which did not suffer itself to be baulked or misled by any pretenses of others." He was "a realist, terrific to all talkers and confused truth-obscuring persons"; he knew no impediment, but was "the agent or attorney of the middle class of modern society," the rising middle class which clutched at wealth and power. "He would steal, slaughter, assassinate, drown and poison as his interest dictated." He was the

119

Ralph Waldo Emerson

prototype of the American man of business. "Never was a leader so endowed," yet he "did all that in him lay to live and thrive without moral principle." That he failed was inevitable, because it was "in the nature of things, the eternal law of man and the world," that enterprises with "sensual and selfish aim," inevitably fail. "Our riches," said Emerson, "will leave us sick; there will be bitterness in our laughter, and our wine will burn our mouths. Only that good profits . . . which serves all men."

Emerson, unlike Faulkner, did not discover the eternal verities among the poor, for he shared with his expansive age the notion that indolence bred poverty, but he did find those verities in the pure in heart. Money was indeed a convenient metaphor which spoke both of the illnesses and the remedies of his time. "Few people," he said, "know how to spend a fine fortune. A beauty of wealth is power without pretension"—this from his journal in 1843. The laws of economy reflect the laws of the world behind which and in which repose transcendent truths. "All things ascend," he affirms in his essay on "Wealth" in 1860, "and the royal rule of economy is that it must ascend also," for "whatever we do must have a higher end." Only he can enrich me, he said, "who can recommend to me the space between sun and sun," making clear yet untold truths.

How remarkably consistent he was. In his sixties, he had not forgotten the young man who some thirty years before had discovered the reality of the God within. "The Divine Mind," he repeated in an 1869 article on "Character" in the *North American Review,* "imparts itself to the single person." Speaking before students at Harvard in 1870, he admitted again his belief "in the existence of the material world as the expression of the spiritual or the real." Returning to the economic metaphor in another article in the *North American Review,* printed only four years before his death, he again confidently affirmed, "Our stock in life, our real estate, is that amount of thought which we have."

The Real Price of Labor

Testing the spirit of his time, he chose to write of wealth and power, for they were words that his generation could understand, but his message remained the same, that wealth or well-being or power comes inevitably to the man who takes advantage of the offerings which nature presents. Those offerings may be small, but to the person who can give himself over to the voice within, they will reveal secrets unforetold. For the real price of labor, of which riches were only a worldly symbol, is knowledge and virtue, available to every man, subject to abuse, but stepping-stones toward wisdom.

R. Waldo Emerson

VIII

The Malady of Partial Reform

EMERSON WAS NOT in any social sense a reformer. He had little patience with the patchwork of partial reformation. The individual was of primary importance: the world and its social and political structures existed only for the benefit of man. Reformation, if it was really to reform, must begin with the single and separate person. Emerson condemned democracy whenever it involved the tyranny of the majority over the individual. He startles a modern reader with an apparent callousness when he says, "Leave this hypocritical prating about the masses. The masses are rude, lame, unmade, pernicious in their demands and influence. . . . Masses! the calamity is the masses. I do not wish any mass at all, but honest men only."

And honest men were rare: "Our politics are full of adventurers," said Emerson, "who having by education and social innocence a good repute in the state, break away from the law of honesty and think they can afford to join the devil's party." In political matters, Emerson assumed the mask of a "wise sceptic." He admitted himself to be a bad citizen who "sees the selfishness of property and the drowsiness of institutions," and is therefore unfit "to work with any democratic party that ever was constituted; for parties wish every one committed," and the independent man "penetrates the popular patriotism."

To many, even among his admirers, Emerson's attitude toward politics has been thought the least attractive thing about him. On the surface, it is harsh and unyielding and chill, lacking communal warmth. "I do not speak often

Ralph Waldo Emerson

to public questions," he apologized in an address on "The Fugitive Slave Law." Private, not public policy was his domain. When occasion required, he could speak out, in a qualified defense of John Brown, on abolition, on the Emancipation Proclamation—good things all, which augured success for the private man. But he had little patience with the reform movements that excited many of his contemporaries. They smoothed surfaces only, and were themselves symptoms of the malady of partial re-formation. "The demon of reform," he called it whose siren voice beguiled, tempting to unmanageable depths: a person must first reform himself.

On this his attitude was unchanging. In an address on "Man the Reformer" in 1841, he insisted, "The duty of every man should be to assume his own vows, should call the institutions of society to account, and examine their fitness to him." What were needed were great men, not institutions petrified nor the tinkering of reform. From this stance, likely to have been as unpopular in his time as it may be in ours, he never varied. Twenty years later, he said, "I have little esteem for governments. . . . I set the private man first." Toward the end of his life, in 1878, speaking of "The Fortune of the Republic," he continued to insist, "What this country longs for is personalities, grand persons, to counteract its materialities." Only they could accomplish true reformation.

Perhaps then the first thing to say about Emerson's politics is that it rises or seems to rise above party affiliation. He is strong in opinion that "politics is a deleterious profession. . . . Men in power have no opinion, but may be had cheap for any opinion, any purpose." He was repelled by "that ill thing, vain and loud, which writes lying newspapers, spouts at caucuses, and sells its lies for gold." However candid his observations, they did not lead him completely to despair. "Things seem to tend downwards," he admitted. They seem to "justify despondency, to promote rogues, to defeat the just; and by knaves as by

The Malady of Partial Reform

martyrs the just cause is carried forward. Although knaves win in every political struggle, although society seems to be delivered over from the hands of one set of criminals into the hands of another set of criminals, as fast as the government is changed, and the march of civilization is a train of felonies,—yet, general aims are somehow answered. . . . Through the years and centuries, through toys and atoms, a great beneficent tendency irresistibly streams."

Whatever hope Emerson discovered for the betterment of mankind gave small attention to people's inclination for minding other people's business. "The less government we have the better," he said. "The State exists only for the education of the wise man," and "with the appearance of the wise man the State expires." Government exists only because man is imperfect, and government is corrupt because man is corrupt. "Good men," said Emerson, "must not obey the law too well."

Emerson avoided regularized partisanship. "We have no sympathy," he said, "with that boyish egotism, hoarse with cheering for one side, for one state, for one town: the right patriotism consists in the delight which springs from contributing our peculiar and legitimate advantages to the benefit of Humanity." Partisanship was cheaply purchased. "Unroof any house," said Emerson, "and you shall find . . . well-being consists in having a sufficiency of coffee and toast, with a daily newspaper, a well glazed parlor, with marbles, mirrors, and centre-tables; and the excitement of a few parties and a few rides in a year. . . . We are shop-keepers," he said. "We peddle, we truck. . . . The customer is the immediate jewel of our souls. Him we flatter, him we feast, compliment, vote for, and will not contradict."

And where do men get their opinions? "Look into the morning trains," invited Emerson, "which, from every suburb, carry the business men into the city and to their shops, counting-rooms, work-yards and warehouses. With them enters the car—the newsboy, the humble priest of politics,

125

Ralph Waldo Emerson

finance, philosophy, and religion. He unfolds his magical sheets—twopence a head his bread of knowledge costs—and instantly the entire rectangular assembly, fresh from their breakfasts, are bending as one man to their second breakfast."

Emerson's observations on politics may seem to apply to other times also, when he says that no political measure "is attempted for itself, but the opinion of the people is courted, in the first place, and the measures are perfunctorily carried through as secondary. We do not choose our candidate, no, nor any other man's choice,—but only the available candidate, whom, perhaps, no one loves. We do not speak what we think, but we grope after the practicable and available. Instead of character, there is a studious exclusion of character. The people are feared and flattered. They are not reprimanded. The country is governed in bar-rooms, and in the mind of bar-rooms. The low can best win the low, and each aspirant for power vies with his rival which can stoop the lowest, and depart widest from himself. . . . We have seen," he continued, "the great party of property and education in the country drivelling, huckstering away . . . every principle of humanity."

Yet for all his attempt at independence, Emerson no more than any other could consistently fail in taking sides. He lived through times which were quickened by large events. In spite of higher realms to which his thought reached, he reacted with justifiable anger against evils of his generation: "The blood is moral: the blood is anti-slavery: it runs cold in the veins: the stomach rises with disgust and curses slavery." He spoke heatedly on the subject. "It was," he said, "the dictate of trade to keep the negro down. We had found a race who were less war-like, and less energetic as shopkeepers than we; who had very little skill in trade. We found it convenient to keep them at work, since, by the aid of a little whipping, we could get their work for nothing." He pointed with unerring consistency at the result of such things. "The mind of this country taught to aim at low

126

objects feeds upon itself." Man stands in his own light; there is little health in him.

Practical politics of the period when Emerson emerged as a writer centered in controversy about the word *democracy*—what was democracy, what characterized the democrat? The word became a shibboleth, as each major party proclaimed itself most truly democratic, and as it attempted to define its conception of the meaning of the word, each party—the Whig and the Democratic—gave expression to contemporary beliefs concerning the relation of the individual to the state, and of individuals to one another.

The membership of the Democrat party, as Emerson knew it, was made up, for the most part, of the poor, the ignorant, and the underprivileged. The conception of democracy that it held seemed to many to have been largely the product of the frontier. It was characterized by a belief in the extension of suffrage, in a desire for territorial expansion at any cost. National expansion would be explained as "Manifest Destiny." Democracy required the right of a majority to control a minority. The attitude prevailing in the Democratic party seemed to reflect dislike for those who had been successful or prosperous, and of suspicion of those who were educated or cultured. The social spirit of the frontier was one of militant egalitarianism, and equality was to be achieved politically by limiting the power of those who were superior, and by denying the merits of the capable, rather than by the development of excellence or culture in the masses. It was levelling, and to men of culture it was dispiriting.

The perceptive young Frenchman, Alexis de Tocqueville, who in the early 1830s visited the United States, described the situation well when a few years later in his account of *Democracy in America* he said, "It cannot be denied that democratic institutions strongly tend to promote the feeling of envy in the human heart; not so much because they afford to everyone the means of rising to the same level with others, as because those means perpetually disappoint the persons who employ them. Democratic institutions awaken and foster a passion for equality which they can never entirely satisfy. . . . The lower orders are agitated by the chance of success, they are irritated by its uncertainty; and they pass from the enthusiasm of pursuit to the exhaustion of ill-success, and lastly to the acrimony of disappointment. Whatever transcends their own limits appears to be an obstacle to their desires, and there is no superiority, however legitimate it may be, which is not irksome in their sight."

If the prevailing attitude of the Democrats was characteristically that of the have-nots, the reverse was true of the Whigs. To the Whig party belonged mainly those who felt that, having succeeded in the attainment of wealth, position, or culture, they must therefore in self-protection preserve the existent political, social, and economic order. Their power seemed threatened in all its aspects by the rising power of the Democrats, who were in the estimation of their opponents the politicians of bar-rooms and cheap newspapers. Many conservatives felt that Jackson's policies would lead to anarchy, and felt that it was the moral obligation of the Whig party to put them down. Distrust of Jacksonian democracy was to a large degree the single unifying bond of the Whig party. For that party was made up of conservatives of different sections of the country, and the local interests of those sections were too diverse to permit a constructive program which could gain the genuine support of the party as a whole. It was mainly, therefore, a party of opposition, and its attitude was negative. The natural consequence was that with the attainment of its primary object by the defeat of its common foe the party disintegrated.

The Whigs, however, like the Democrats, proclaimed great belief in democracy. They maintained that in its republican form, the government of the United States was inherently democratic, insofar at least as it had been

The Malady of Partial Reform

founded in opposition to monarchy. "The people of the United States are democratic, and it is to be hoped they always will be," wrote the Whig historian Calvin Colton in 1846. "Did they not declare and achieve independence, to be rid of regal power?" It was this antimonarchial interpretation of democracy which the Whigs relied upon to justify their stand against Jackson, whom they denounced as a demagogic tyrant.

The Whigs believed that political power should be in the hands of those who were wisest and best, who in a spirit of *noblesse oblige* would rule in the best interest of all. In advocating this belief, they insisted that they were truly democratic; in fact, they occasionally proclaimed themselves disciples of Jefferson. But they did not believe with the Democrats in unrestricted majority rule: "The point they were always endeavoring to make," wrote an English observer, "was to confide power to comparatively few, and to deprive the masses of the privilege of voting." But, this aside, there was little difference between the abstract political ideas advanced by the two parties. "It is remarkable," observed Harriet Martineau when she visited the United States in the mid-1830s, "how nearly their positive statements of political doctrine agree, while they differ in almost every possible application of their common principles." To understand Emerson's political sympathies, it is necessary, therefore, to observe his attitude toward actual parties, rather than at his use of words which were common to both parties.

His essay on "Politics," though fundamental, is likely to be misleading in this respect. Any political system, he there says, is an institution, man-made—"all are imitable, all alterable; we may make as good, we may make better." The laws that govern states, he said, are only memorandums. "We are superstitious, and esteem the statute somewhat," forgetting that it only lives in the activity of strong men who give it force: "Our statute," said Emerson

129

Ralph Waldo Emerson

"is a currency which we stamp with our own portrait: it soon becomes unrecognizable, and in process of time will return to the mint." One who looks behind the appearances of his day to fact which is grounded in eternal truth discovers that "Nature is not democratic, not limited-monarchial, but despotic." Her laws are absolute, man's laws are relative. Yet, on the temporal level, man must live by his laws—only being careful to discard what is outmoded, to rephrase according to the insights of present perception.

"Of persons," he says, "all have equal rights, in virtue of being identical in nature. This interest of course with its whole power demands a democracy." Yet, though "the rights of all as persons are equal, in virtue of their access to Reason, their rights in property are very unequal. One man owns his clothes, and another man owns a county." According to Whig doctrine, the man who owns a county is a better man. Here it is, Emerson recognizes, that democratic theory splits into two segments: "Personal rights, universally the same, demand a government framed on the ratio of the census; property demands a government framed on the ratio of owners and of owning."

Ideally, abstractly, he was on the first side. "Democracy, Freedom," he said, "has its root in the sacred truth that every man hath in him the divine Reason, or that, though few men since the creation of the world live according to the dictates of Reason, yet all men are capable of so doing. . . . That is the equality and the only equality of all men." The responsibility of America, said Emerson, "is to liberate, to abolish kingcraft, priestcraft, caste, monopoly; to pull down the gallows, to burn up the bloody statute book, to take the immigrant, to open the doors of the sea and the fields of the earth."

But great actions demanded great men, and these the party called Democratic Emerson feared could not supply: "They have not at heart the ends which give to the name of democracy what hope and virtue are in it. The spirit of our American radicalism is destructive and aimless; it is

The Malady of Partial Reform

not loving; it has no ulterior and divine ends, but is destructive only." Of the two parties, the Democrats and the Whigs, the first, he said, "has the best cause, and the other contains the best men." And men are greater than parties: "The root and seed of democracy," he wrote in his journals, "is the doctrine, Judge for yourself. Reverence yourself. It is the inevitable effect of the doctrine, where it has any effect (which is rare), to insulate the partisan, to make each man a state. At the same time, it replaces the dead with a living check in a true, delicate reverence for superior, congenial minds."

"When I speak of the democratic element," he cautioned, "I do not mean that ill thing, vain and loud, which writes lying newspapers, spouts at caucuses, and sells its lies for gold." "There is nothing," he said again, "of the true democratic element in what is called Democracy; it must fall, being wholly commercial." It is notorious, he said "that the Jackson party is the *Bad* party in the cities and in general in the country." He speaks of its "unmixed malignity, . . . withering selfishness, . . . impudent vulgarity."

Nor was Emerson's quarrel with the Democrats confined to the Jackson era. In an entry in his journal headed "Van Burenism," he wrote, "I passed by the shop and saw my spruce neighbor, the dictator of our rural Jacobins, teaching his little circle of villagers their political lessons. And here, thought I, is one who loves what I hate. . . . I hate persons who are nothing but persons. I hate numbers. He cares for nothing but numbers and persons." And as with Van Buren, so with his successors. Polk and Cass were more powerful than Webster or Clay, thought Emerson, because they stood nearer the rum barrel.

Emerson eventually opposed the ideas of the Democrats as well as the personality of their leaders. In 1842 he wrote: "Since I have been here in New York I have grown less diffident of my political opinions. I supposed once the Democracy must be right." Now, "I see they are aimless."

It asks for freedom, he wrote a year later, "but for what? Only for freedom; not to any noble end." The annexation of Texas and the Mexican War which resulted from it were regarded by conservative New Englanders as Democratic plots to extend slavery and the influence of their party. They had the votes on their side, but they were wrong; and Emerson came at length to deny and anathematize the central tenet of the Democratic party. "Majorities," he described as "the argument of fools, the strength of the weak." He now believed, "A few foolish . . . managers ride the conscience of this great country with their Texas . . . or Democracy, or other mumbo-jumbo, and all . . . are verily persuaded that that is great. . . . And why? Because there is really no great life."

Great life, great men, self-reliant and independent, were what Emerson demanded, and he found none among his contemporaries. Even the Whig party, "composed of the most moderate, able, and cultivated part of the population, is timid," he said. "It vindicates no right, aspires to no real good." In England in 1847, he found things very different: "A manly ability, a general sufficiency, is the genius of the English. . . . a man is a man here,—a quite costly and respectable production, in his own and in other eyes." On his return he referred to America as "the Paradise of the third class; . . . England," he said, "is the paradise of the first class."

His idealism was tempered now by experience—yet it remained throughout idealism still. It was a year after his visit abroad that he exploded, "Leave this hypocritical prating about masses," they "need not to be flattered but to be schooled." Rather than concede to them, he would "tame, drill, divide and break them up, and draw individualism out of them." He again seems callous, as he says, "The worst of charity is that the lives you are asked to preserve are not worth preserving. Masses! the calamity is the masses! I do not wish any mass at all, but honest men only, lively, sweet, accomplished women only. . . . In old Egypt it was estab-

132

The Malady of Partial Reform

lished law that the vote of a prophet be reckoned equal to a hundred hands. I think it was much underestimated."

If a younger Emerson believed that the Democrats might have some superior ideas, his attitude changed, as a result of renewed Democratic successes after the 1840s and the agitation over Texas, slavery and the Mexican War, so that he became skeptical of the whole party and its ideas. During the decades of the 1850s and thereafter, his skepticism increased to the point that he doubted the efficacy of democracy of any kind, whether as represented by a party or as an idea; it is during this latter period that he denounced even more strongly such tenets of American democratic faith as belief in the virtue of the masses and majority rule. He speaks on politics now much as H. L. Mencken, who ridiculed other aspects of Emerson's thought, would speak in the next century, caustically condemning the masses whose thoughts and votes were controlled by demagogues.

Yet he never departed from his central assumption, that "governments have their origin in the moral identity of men." He continued to insist that the touchstone of a truly successful political system was that it bred great individuals, and that it be devoted to moral ends. "The end of all political struggle," he said in one of his last lectures—at the Old South Church in Boston in 1878—"is to establish morality as the basis of all legislation. 'Tis not free institutions, 'tis not democracy that is the end,—no, only the means. Morality is the object of government. . . . The highest end of government is the culture of men." It should be in the hands of those who were superior in intellect, in morality. He argued that "the terrible aristocracy that is in Nature" operates in favor of the production of excellence. Superior men—like Daniel Webster, John Brown, or Abraham Lincoln, three of Emerson's American heroes—are sure to surpass others by the very fact of their superiority. Emergency would inevitably bring them forward as it had brought Lincoln forward. "A fire breaking out in a village makes immediately a natural government. The most able and energetic take the command, and are gladly obeyed by the rest."

The emergency of war presented itself three times during Emerson's life. The first, the war of 1812, he watched as a boy, with a boy's enthusiasm for noble deeds, writing shrill patriotic verses with his schoolmates. The second, the Mexican War, was part of a demagogic plot, immoral in every sense; democracy had become "a government of bullies tempered by editors." He saw now "the reckless and destructive fury which characterizes the lower classes of American society, . . . pampered by hundreds of profligate presses," and recognized the evils perpetrated by "young intriguers who drive in bar-rooms and town meetings the trade of politics" and "have put the country in the position of an overgrown bully." The Civil War was a righteous war; to it he offered what talents he had, in speaking and contributing to relief committees. "Like the rest of us," said Nathaniel Hawthorne, "even the mild Mr. Emerson" began "now breathing fire."

But he never felt the reality of that war as Melville or Whitman did. He saw it from afar as something noble: "The shame of living seems taken away," he said. This internecine war was a judgment upon a sinful people. "Let it search, let it grind, let it overrun," he said. "We do not often," he said, "have a moment of grandeur in these hurried, slipshod, aimless lives." When the slaughter was over, he told a Harvard assembly that the new era it promised was "worth the lives of all this generation of American men, if they had been demanded."

The war affected Emerson strongly—perhaps because he participated in it as a middle-aged encourager rather than as a participant. It was a frightening test of his idealism. A new age was emerging in which he seemed to have no part. But unlike his younger contemporaries, Melville and Hawthorne and Thoreau, each of whom rose to climactic greatness in the 1850s, and progressed little farther, Emerson

The Malady of Partial Reform

clung to his ideals and spoke them even to an unattentive audience.

It is the younger Emerson who is perhaps more attractive —he who in the late 1830s found war "an epidemic insanity, breaking out here and there like the cholera or influenza, infecting men's brains instead of their bowels"; who was sure that it was "the ignorant and childish part of mankind that is the fighting part," that it was the result of "idle and vacant minds," of men whose "animal nature alone has been developed." He looked then to a nation of men "risen to that height of moral cultivation that they will not declare war or carry arms, for they have not so much madness in their brains." He called for a Congress of Nations then, through which man might harmoniously work out differences with other men. "Nations," he said, "are made to help each other as families were; and all advancement is by ideas, and not by brute force or mechanic power."

When he suggested that a single human being might steadily deny the authority of laws, on the simple ground of his own moral nature, he anticipated Thoreau's remarks on civil disobedience, which anticipate Mahatma Ghandi's campaign of passive resistance and the crusade of Martin Luther King, Jr., for human justice. And when he observed late in his life that "our sleepy civilization, ever since Roger Bacon and Monk Schwartz invented gunpowder, has built its whole art of war . . . on that one compound . . . as if the earth, water, gases, lightning and caloric had not a million energies, the discovery of any one of which could change the art of war," he was being prophetic indeed. "Don't trust children with edged tools. Don't trust man," he advised, "with more power than he has until he has learned to use that little better. What a hell we would make of the world if we could do what we would!"

We today may believe ourselves to have discovered too much, however, of human motives, including our own, to respond completely to the young Emerson who called for "the power of love, as the basis of a State," who looked forward to "a nation of lovers, of benefactors, or true, great and able men; . . . men of love, honor, and truth; men of an immense industry; men whose influence is felt to the end of the earth." This younger Emerson called for men of principle rather than of passion, men devoted "no longer to the service of the individual but to the common soul of all men." "The cause of peace," he said, "is not the cause of cowardice. . . . If peace is to be maintained, it must be by brave men" who will stake their lives for principle. They will search "the sublime laws of morals and the sources of hope and trust, in man, and not in books, in the present, not in the past." Then, he said, "war has a short day and human blood will cease to flow."

"Democracy, Freedom has its roots in the sacred truth," he wrote in an early journal, "that every man has in him the divine Reason," the ability to listen to the voice of the God within. "That is the equality and only equality of all men." Institutions perish; social or political reform flares brightly for a moment, and through the agency of a great person may momentarily succeed, but lacking such leadership it will sputter into a thousand sparks which fail to ignite; well-meaning charity can unman the person it intends to aid. Emerson spoke to his expansive time of financial and political brigandage when in 1878 he declared forcefully again that what was wanted was "men of original perception and original action, . . . men of elastic and moral mind, who can live in the moment and take a step forward." For the "end of all political struggle is to establish morality as the basis of legislation. 'Tis not free institutions, 'tis not democracy that is the end,—no, but only the means." His voice still rings true as he continued, "Morality is the end of government."

IX

Illusion and Reality

E MERSON GREW with his times. What has seemed
to some commentators a change in attitude from the
early 1840s when he confidently celebrated the infinitude of
the private man, the immanence of spirit, and the sufficiency
of nature, to the period of the 1850s and 1860s when he is
said to have stood less confidently on these premises, is
largely illusionary. As America grew, he grew with it. Experience, personal and public, increased his certainty that
nature, whatever its beneficence, could be cruel and often
offered alluring temptations toward rapacity. The death of
his first son was an extension of the same natural ruthless-
ness which had left him an orphan at ten, had taken from
him his two brilliant brothers and his adored first wife.
Disaster in many guises still lurked threatening, menacing
and perverting. The temper of his time—western land
grabs, the annexation of Texas, the Mexican War, the Gold
Rush, all seemed to give the lie to his assurance that wealth
derived from excellence. Slavery was an abrupt affront to
his assurance of the essential equality of all men. When
Daniel Webster in 1850 voted against the Fugitive Slave
Law, Emerson was saddened that even the apparently greatest of men could be misdirected by forces too powerful to
withstand.

Emerson recognized the maladies of his times, the misap-
propriation of wealth and power, the lack of greatness of
spirit for which he called. Though not of what has been
called the Party of Doubt, made up of people like his
neighbor Nathaniel Hawthorne whose writings, Emerson

once said, "were not good for anything," presumably because they were not sufficiently instructive, and like Herman Melville, a younger man, whose iconoclastic view of the world could never be quite brought to focus, Emerson was as hard-headed, with as clear a view of public and private insufficiencies, as either of these. By the time they were creating their fables of remonstrance, he was also taking his countrymen to task for sins of omission and commission.

His writing of the decade of the 1850s stands more sturdily than has often been recognized among the great works of what has been called the American Renaissance—Hawthorne's *The Scarlet Letter* in 1850, Melville's *Moby-Dick* in 1851, Thoreau's *Walden* in 1854, and Walt Whitman's *Leaves of Grass* in 1855. Less often read than his ebullient essays of the 1840s, Emerson's contributions to the literature of the following decade speak even more explicitly of the malaise of his time than any of his traditionally more celebrated contemporaries. His view of the world was as tough-minded, perhaps even more clear-sighted, than any of these others. It came to first climax in *Representative Men* in 1850, just as the Renaissance began. Heightened by experience abroad, it was intensified and expanded in *English Traits* in 1856. *The Conduct of Life* in 1860 capsulated and stated with explicit plainness thoughts which he had been formulating for almost thirty years.

The difference between Emerson and most of these others was that he maintained an intellectual ground plan upon which he consistently built. His certainty of the infinitude of the private person, the individual, though sorely tried, remained unchanged. Of course, with experience he grew: he saw, suffered, and grieved. The world in which he was doomed to live was not the world which it might be, or which might through his influence become. He recognized as clearly as any of his contemporaries the traps that nature laid for human frailty: among her manifold gifts was recognition of peril and terror, the odious aspects of life, the

snares set for the unwary, the attractive lures of dissipation, the temptations which interfered with concentration.

Emerson searched for and he argued for and submitted
recipes for greatness in people, urging a single-minded,
personally controlled attention to what each could become.
And he never forsook that quest. He grew as few of his contemporaries grew, circling ever more widely from the center
which he had identified when at thirty-four he published his
first small book on *Nature*. There was no essential change,
only expansion. Except for Thoreau, who took early direction from him, Emerson, more than these others of his time,
had ground to stand on. His thought derived not only from
active tradition handed down by his long line of clerical ancestors, but also from intellectual currents from Europe and
the Orient. He was both among the most native and the most
cultivated cosmopolitans of his century.

His two years abroad in the late 1840s revealed not new,
but expanded views of deficiencies among people. Across the
Atlantic, he found much the same world that he had left
behind, a world "of cake and ale, of men and truth and
folly." The French were immoral; the Spaniards and Italians
were so caught within codified institutions of church and
state that they had become intellectually retrospective, un-
willing and unable to advance; the Irish were servile, almost
as if willingly downtrodden; but the English, though debili-
tated by inherited restrictions, were in many respects worthy
of emulation. Emerson was by nurture and conviction a
white Anglo-Saxon Protestant, with many, if not all, of the
convictions and prejudices of that class.

His attitude toward race may to a twentieth-century
reader be another unattractive aspect of his thought. Slavery
was an abomination, but he nonetheless was confident that
blacks, like Indians, Spaniards, or Italians, because of their
temperament and condition, were incapable of creating truly
great persons. Human greatness needed freedom, as much
from codified tradition as from bondage. Emerson's back-

ground and experience suggested that this freedom was most likely to be found in his time among people of Saxon heritage. Released from subjugation to priest, master, or superstition, these others might emerge toward greatness, as had the ancient Greeks, the prophets of Israel, or the mystics of India, but not, Emerson believed, in his time.

It was, he at one time thought, the patterned aristocracy of England, where cultivated people lived balanced lives, dressing for dinner, ritually passing port wine to the left, suavely polite, that presented to him an approximate but finally superficial model of what people might be. He admired the caste organization of English society. It was as attractive, he thought, as the wonderful diversity of the English countryside. Polished and accomplished people were to be found among those of the English nobility who were beginning to spread their tentacles of power over the world. But their position was inherited, a gift from the past; their power was over people, not nature. Emerson failed finally to discover among them the new man for whom he sought; he found instead only replicas of past greatness. They were comfortable, and it was comfortable to be with them, but Emerson did not meet any among them, he said, who were truly great or even consistently interesting.

Industry, which discovered and exploited new harnessings of nature, was producing in England, as well as in America, a new breed—rapacious, self-seeking only in a worldly sense, but who with practical sense utilized nature in a manner that most of the aristocratic class had forgotten or neglected. Emerson, admiring, critical, and finally disappointed, swung backwards and forwards in his attitude toward the English, who so successfully made the best of what their small island provided. He found "the Englishman to be him of all men who stands firmest in his shoes. . . . Each man walks, eats, drinks, shaves, dresses, gesticulates, and, in every manner, acts and suffers without reference to bystanders, in his own fashion." Superficially, they were the most self-reliant of people: "Every man in this polished country consults only his own convenience, as much as a solitary pioneer in Wisconsin." Yet it was a wasted land which would finally be unable to compete with its sons and daughters who had emigrated to the New World. As he left them, Emerson told his English hosts, "I will go back to the capes of Massachusetts and my own Indian stream, and say to my countrymen, the old race are all gone, and the elasticity and hope of mankind must henceforth remain on the Allegheny ranges, or nowhere."

To appreciate the extent to which Emerson kept pace with his times, it is thus helpful to read his *English Traits*, published in 1856, only a year after Whitman's *Leaves of Grass*. For *English Traits* is in large part an exuberant extension of Emerson's pronouncements in his early *Essays*. He had continued to move in circles outward from his central position, and this Whitman might have discovered if he had read Emerson's *Representative Men*, which was published five years before Whitman's great self-celebrating poem appeared. In that volume Emerson celebrated not himself or any other native son, but rather looked abroad and to the past for examples of the human greatness which over many years he had sought and attempted to describe. Whitman's third edition of *Leaves of Grass* in 1860 was to Emerson quite too explicit in its celebration of physical attraction among people. His own quietly explicit *The Conduct of Life,* published in the same year, celebrated nothing: it was a painstakingly plainspoken exposition wrapped tightly around the core of what he had been saying for almost thirty years.

The Conduct of Life was Emerson's last significant volume, and appeared not only in the same year as Whitman's splendid, to many people the best, edition of *Leaves of Grass,* but also Hawthorne's last significant book, *The Marble Faun.* With these three books the American Renaissance came to an end. A Civil War was brewing that would divide the nation, and during wartime great literature is not likely to be produced. Emerson, like Whitman, would write sorrow-

Ralph Waldo Emerson

fully on the death of Lincoln, but after the war directions in literature were changed by new writers who, in the large, turned their backs on their prewar predecessors. Emerson continued to write, almost until his death in 1882. He collected his poems twice, in 1867 and 1876; *Society and Solitude* in 1870 tells almost as much in title as in content; *Fortune of the Republic* in 1878 seems more petulant than persuading. After the war between the states, Emerson's country moved with faster pace than he could maintain. But what he had said lived on, as influence and inspiration.

The Conduct of Life can be thought of as an ethical guide or a practical handbook on how to get along in a world that seems not always to be constructed according to a person's liking. It is here that Emerson speaks of wealth and power as proper rewards that, when well used, are beneficial, but, when ill used, a bane. He speaks of a person's duty toward other persons, but particularly of the person's duty to himself, in self reliant use of whatever abilities he has. His stance throughout much of the book is that of a pragmatic man among men, addressing himself to matters subject to immediate improvement. What change there is from his earlier writings is more in expression than substance.

Years before, a fumbling young Emerson, unsure of his vocation, asked "What shall be the substance of my shrift?" His answer had been that he would view the world as if he were seeing it for the first time and honestly report what he had seen. That having been done, he asked now another question, which is, "How shall I live?" He admitted inability to solve all public questions—the "riddle of the world has for each a private solution." His faith confidently remained on the single, separate person, however hedged about by "immovable limitations" that render him "Incompetent . . . to span the huge orbits of prevailing ideas, behold their return and reconcile their opposition," but committed to the trial.

If a conduct book, it is a curious conduct book indeed.

Illusion and Reality

Sandwiched between an introductory chapter on "Fate" and a concluding chapter on "Illusions" are seven chapters which are concerned with such practical matters as "Power," "Wealth," "Culture," "Behavior," "Worship," then a by-path chapter on "Considerations by the Way," preceding a penultimate chapter on "Beauty," all of which, to one degree or another, are subject to fate and distorted by illusion. Emerson echoes now what Melville had said in *Mardi* eleven years before about the unseemly braggadocio of America: "Let me honestly state the facts," he said. "Our America has a bad name for superficialness. Great men, great nations, have not been boasters or buffoons, but perceivers of the terror of life, and have manned themselves to face it."

It is in "Fate" that Emerson declares the world "rough and surly," admits that it conceals "ferocities in the interiors of nature," and speaks of "the rough and incalculable road" followed by that "terrific benefactor" called providence. He insists, "No picture of life can have any veracity that does not admit the odious facts." Fate is fate, inexorably present: "when each comes forth from his mother's womb, the gate of gifts closes behind him." He is what he is: "He has but one future and that already predetermined," by heredity, by environment, according to the talents which nature has allowed.

He speaks plainly now as he declares that the power of any person "is hooped by necessity, which, by many experiments, he touches on every side until he knows its arc." Limitation is the rule, expansion the ideal. Among "certain men sex and digestion absorb the vital force, and the stronger these are the individual is so much weaker," satisfied to remain a creature of circumstance. "Most men and women are just one couple more," never knowing that, though fate is powerful, one part of its immensity is the freedom of man. But then with remarkable consistency he says again what for years he had been saying, "So long as a man thinks, he is free. . . . The revelation of thought takes man out of servitude into freedom." Only mind, guided by

insight and perception, can attack the seemingly impregnable
stronghold of fate, which is only another name "for facts not
yet proved under the fire of thought; for causes which are
unpenetrated."

Stumbling from error to error, unthinking man falls
exhausted into lassitude, baffled by the apparent merciless
savagery of nature. Its ordinances are severe and, as Emerson
had first said in his essay on *Nature* almost a quarter of a
century before, demand discipline. Nature requires self-
knowledge and humility. Expanding again what he had said
almost twenty years earlier in "Compensation," Emerson
now again explains that every person "must thank his de-
fects, and stand in some awe of his talents," discovering that
"evil is good in the making," that "weights have wings."
Though small indeed beside the immensity of nature, though
wounded by accident of birth or circumstance, a person
need not flounder rudderless. He has eyes to see and mind to
penetrate into nature's guarded secrets. His "day of days,
the great day of the feast of life, is that in which the inward
eye opens to the Unity of thing. . . . A man speaking from
insight affirms of himself what is true of the mind: seeing its
immortality, he says, I am immortal; seeing its invincibility,
he says, I am strong."

Though "the knot of nature," he said, "is so well tied that
nobody was ever cunning enough to find the two ends,"
Nature is "intricate, overlapped, interweaved and endless,"
but behind the "circle of animal life,—tooth against tooth,
devouring war, the war for food, a yelp of pain and a grunt
of triumph, there is immeasurable unity." In man, "every
generosity, every new perception, the love and praise he
exhorts from his fellows, are certificates of advance out of
fate into freedom. Liberation of the will from the sheaths
and clogs of organization which he has outgrown, is the aim
and end of this world." History "is the action and reaction
of . . . Nature and Thought; two boys pushing each other
on the curbstone of the pavement. Everything is pusher or

pushed; and matter and mind are in perpetual tilt and balance."

In "Power" Emerson plays counterpoint to what he has already said of "Fate." "The key to all ages," he suggests, "is—imbecility: imbecility in the vast majority of men at all times and even in heroes in all but certain eminent moments; victims of gravity, custom, and fear. This gives force to the strong,—that the multitude have no habit of self-reliance or original action." Power feeds on the sickness of society, on people who are not reliant, who fail to be whole by taking advantage of what talent they have been allowed. Misdirected or misapplied, power can be a terrifying evil. Applied with intelligence it can produce immense advantage. Steam can blow a man to pieces or bring him immeasurable benefit. Either way, power is present; it is there, a part of fate, waiting to direct or be directed by man.

"The one prudence of life is concentration; the one evil dissipation; and it makes no difference whether the dissipations are coarse or fine: property and its cares, friends and a social habit, or politics, or music, or feasting. Everything is good which takes away one plaything and delusion more and drives home to add one stroke of faithful work. . . . You must elect your work; you shall take what your brain can, and drop all the rest. Only so can the amount of vital force accumulate which can make the step from knowing to doing." Power finds expression in action, in moving, not without thought, but through thought to accomplishment, which is partial because man is partial and his thinking circumscribed by circumstance. And power, because immense, must be handled with care. It can lift to dazzling heights or it can destroy. Emerson speaks disdainfully of the "worthlessness of amateurs" who neglect their opportunity to pierce nature's cryptic guises and discover truths certified as eternal.

Ralph Waldo Emerson

"Wealth" is an inevitable concomitant of power, subject to abuse, but providing possibilities for great good when spent "in spiritual creation and not in augmenting animal existence." "Culture" explains what can be done with the benefits which wealth in goods or character supply. Emerson speaks again of books and travel and other methods of self-improvement. He distinguishes between egotism and self-reliance. One of the most annoying forms that egotism can take is a craving for sympathy: "The sufferers parade their miseries, tear the lint from their bruises, reveal their indictable crimes, that you may pity them. They like sickness, because physical pain will extort some show of interest from the bystanders." Although this "goitre of egotism" is perhaps necessary for the preservation of the species, as begging is necessary for the preservation of beggars, it is destructive of self-respect. It is pretentious, and a representative American foible. In "Culture," he defines the "mark of the man of the world" as "absence of pretension. He does not make a speech; he takes a low business-tone, avoids all brag, is nobody, dresses plainly, promises not at all, performs much, speaks in monosyllables, hugs his fact." Let us learn "to live coarsely, dress plainly, and lie hard. . . . Response and cheerfulness are the badge of the gentleman—repose in energy."

All of this had been said before. At the end of his effective career Emerson attempted to make clear what he had for so many years been saying, seeking more homely, practical terms with which to express it to a new, more hard-headed generation. His center remained firm, but his radiation from it took now more worldly directions. The challenge was to demonstrate that though times might change, truth was changeless. And readers responded to this most plainly expressed yet most subtly insinuating of his books.

Suburban life such as Emerson lived was, he told them, superior to urban life. Although cities were "centres where the best things are found," whether in opera, theater, museum, or shop, they finally "degrade us by magnifying trifles." There dwell "a supple, glib-tongued tribe, who live for show, servile to public opinion. Life is dragged down to a fracas of pitiful cares and disasters. . . . Keep the town," he advises, "for occasions." Retreat to quietness is as necessary for health as for power: "He who would inspire and lead his race must be defended from traveling with the souls of other men, from living, breathing, reading and writing in the daily, time-worn yoke of their opinions. . . . Every brave heart will treat society as a child, and never allow it to dictate."

In "Behavior," he speaks mainly of manners, which "are the happy ways of doing things," creating "a rich varnish with which the routine of life is washed and its details adorned." Social grace is a healthful adornment of the Spirit. He reverts with confidence to one of his earliest certainties as he explains, "The basis of all good manners is self-reliance, . . . those who are not self-possessed obtrude and pain us." We are uncomfortable with them because they are uncomfortable with us. The cultivation of manners "requires time, as nothing is more vulgar than haste. Friendship should be surrounded with ceremonies and respects, and not crushed in corners." And love also. Above all else sincerity is required: "What is done for effect is seen to be done for effect; and what is done for love is felt to be done for love." Society provides "the stage on which manners are shown; novels are their literature. Novels are the journal or record of manners." They are "useful as Bibles if they teach you the secret that the best life is conversation, and the greatest success is confidence, or perfect understanding between sincere people." For superior people are direct, not subtle; they are sincere, concealing nothing, "not facile, apologetic, or leaky," but "in every gesture or action shall indicate power at rest."

Manners may thus become more than ritual because they identify the self-reliant man. And "Worship" also may be more than ritual: "God builds his temple in the heart on the ruins of churches and religions. . . . The cure for false theology is mother-wit. Forget your books and traditions," he admonished, "and obey your moral principles at this hour." The fatal defect of his time Emerson thought to be "the divorce between religion and morality." Learn, he advised, that the "true meaning of *spiritual* is *real*"; know that "the Spirit does not love cripples and malformations," but whole men, thinking; recognize that the "religion which is to guide and fulfill the present and coming ages, whatever else it be, must be intellectual."

Emerson is approaching again to the heart of his doctrine, the reality of spirit. He pauses for an essay which he calls "Considerations by the Way" in which he talks wisely of a number of things, to conclude again that "the escape from all false ties; courage to be what we are, and love of what is simple and beautiful; independence and cheerful relation, these are the essentials,—these, and the wish to serve, to add somewhat to the well-being of men." He turns then to an essay on "Beauty," in which with characteristic ambiguity he talks of science, in reminder that the man of science penetrates as directly toward the harmonies of nature as the poet or painter, to discover with them that "all high beauty has a moral element in it."

Finally he turns to contemplation of "Illusions," a subject not new. In the essay on "Experience" in 1844, he had warned: "Dream delivers us to dream, and there is no end to illusion. Life is a train of moods, like a string of beads, and as we pass through them they prove to be many-colored lenses which paint the world their own hue." In "Prudence" he warned again that "the world of sense is a world of shows; it does not exist for itself, but has a symbolic character"; and in an essay on "Montaigne" he admitted that "knowledge is the knowing that we cannot know." Now he states even more firmly that all men are "victims of illusion in all parts of life. Children, youths, adults and old men, all are

Illusion and Reality

led by one bauble or another"; life is a "riddle, and the key to a riddle is another riddle. There are as many pillows of illusion as flakes in a snow-storm. We wake from one dream into another dream. The toys to be sure are various, and are graduated in refinement to the quality of the dupe. The intellectual man requires a fine bait; but sots are easily amused. But everybody is drugged by his own frenzy, and the pageant marches at all hours, with music and banner and badge."

He begins lightly: "Women more than all, are the element and kingdom of illusion. Being fascinated, they fascinate." Marriage is a lure of nature, "a special trap . . . laid to trip up our feet with, and all are tripped up first or last." There is the illusion of love, the illusion of time, the illusion of special calling and of miracle, the illusion that the sun travels about the earth, and the illusion of beauty. Nature is jealous of her secrets; coyly she strips off but one veil at a time as she reveals glimpses of herself to man. To imagine that she can ever be known completely is the greatest of all illusions. In its material manifestations, the world is a wondrous mystery, thrilling with fleeting intimations of its secrets as natural facts become shadowed symbols of spiritual facts.

"In this kingdom of illusions," says Emerson, "we grope eagerly for stays and foundations." We know that with time and experience we may know more than we once did, or we have the illusion that we do, and so we imagine we may sometime know more. Yet the only reality is oneself—and not the self which is ordinarily shown to other people, for that too is a facade, an illusive product of their imagination or one's own. What can be truly known—and even then perhaps not fully apprehended—is the spirit within which is the only reality. Shadows of illusion that blur each person's perception may perhaps be pragmatically useful, but are ultimately destructive of the person's inlet to truth. In the world of sense, illusion rules supreme.

Ralph Waldo Emerson

Emerson is a dualist only in that he recognizes matter as the vehicle or shadow of the spirit. What can truly be known amid the terrifying and beautiful and invigorating and tantalizingly tempting varicolored and many-faceted series of illusions amid which each person must live is the reality of spirit. However delusive are appearances, "Whatever games are played with us, we must play no games with ourselves, but deal in our privacy with the last honesty and truth." No one can comprehend nor finally assist a person but himself. The share of spirit which is within each is the center about which the universe moves. Every person's perception, when honest and direct, unclouded by illness, want, or rapacity, will lead out of himself to enough understanding of the world to circumvent its dangers and live as satisfyingly as possible among illusions that allure.

Only the spirit is immortal, "not mine, nor thine," Emerson continued to insist, but a part of an eternal whole, shared by all. It cannot be coerced, but stands servant and master to people who will listen to its voice, discovering within themselves hints of immortal truths that inspire human excellence. He concluded now that "life is a series of dreams, yet poetic justice is done in dreams also. The visions of good men are good; it is the undisciplined will that is whipped with bad thoughts and bad fortunes."

The key to life conducted well is character, which is formed by intelligent apprehension of the proper uses of power, wealth, culture, behavior, worship, and beauty of which Emerson has spoken, all subject to limitation by fate and prey to illusion. It was not to be found in people in mass, but in the single separate person. "I do not wish any mass at all," Emerson had said in "Considerations by the Way." He wanted "honest men only, lovely, sweet, accomplished women" of integrity and sincerity. "I look," he said as the book ended, "upon the simple and childish virtues of veracity and honesty as the root of all that is sublime in character. Speak as you think, be what you are, pay your debts of all kinds. . . . This reality is the foundation of friendship, religion, poetry and art. At the top or bottom of all illusions, I set the cheat which leads us to work and live for appearances; in spite of our conviction, in all sane hours, that it is which we really are that avails, with friends, with strangers, and with fate or fortune."

The ultimate consistent simplicity of Emerson recognizes a soiled world, misdirected by man's best gifts of well-being and power. He knew as much of the obscene multiplicity of evil as either William Faulkner or Jean-Paul Sartre, and his recipe for cure was much the same as theirs: simplicity, honesty, humility, faith in what is best in oneself. Ernest Hemingway's *The Old Man and the Sea*—in which, said Faulkner, Hemingway speaks about God—is a fable in more modern terms that celebrates similar virtues, with not unsimilar warnings. Existentialism, which seems to say that only being—which is terrifying and stimulating and sometimes masked with illusion of loveliness—is immortal, moves only in words beyond Emerson. Existence is immortal; the spirit that breathes being is immortal; explanatory insight of ultimate accessibility is immortal.

Our debt to Emerson is best paid, however, not when we discover in writers of our century or even in ourselves formulations that resemble his, but when, convinced, perhaps by illusion, that we have moved beyond him, we think our own thoughts and try our own skill at untying the intricate knots of truth, recognizing him as a father to be repudiated, but who, in coalescing traditions from our common past, provides a platform on which to stand as we do it.

X

The Mark of Greatness

A S *The Conduct of Life* in 1860 has been said to mark the end of the surge of literary activities that in the 1850s brought forth the writings of Hawthorne, Melville, Whitman, and Thoreau, so Emerson's *Representative Men* of 1850 can be thought of as marking its beginning. It posed in different terms, from a different angle of vision, both the visionary and iconoclastic aspects of that mid-century decade. What has been called the American Renaissance begins and ends with Emerson. If he has not the great white mysterious whale of Melville, the ambiguous scarlet letter of Hawthorne, the small house by a pond of Thoreau, nor the bold barbaric yawp of Whitman, his writings nonetheless provide the frame within which these are displayed.

His concern, like theirs, was a consideration of how a person may confront the ideals, idiosyncracies, and perils of a rapidly expanding, avaricious, yet well-meaning young nation. The choices were various. One could withdraw from it, could celebrate it vauntingly, could masquerade it subtly in garments of the past, or plunge recklessly into symbolic representation of whale and walls and wounded men. None of these was Emerson's way. His response to the spirit of those turbulent times was more quietly and more directly spoken. He understood the perils and pitfalls that threatened. He knew of want and cruelty and avariciousness and deception as well as any of these others. But he held his head high, searching beyond the present. What, he asked, is not for my time only, but for all time the distinguishing mark of human greatness? Is redemption truly possible?

Ralph Waldo Emerson

If not wealth, if not power, if not the satisfaction of solitude or the comfort of society, what is it that identifies the
truly fulfilled individual? Emerson's confidence in the infinitude of the private person and of possibilities for self-
sufficiency in all people ran headlong into observation, long
held, that some enjoyed superiority denied to others. How
then is one to achieve true greatness? How, finally, is a
person made whole? Wherein lies the salvation sought by all?

What is more natural among competitive people than a
yearning for superiority? The yearning may be diminished or
may disappear in despair. As Emerson had earlier explained,
every person is partial, is wounded physically, morally, intellectually. At his birth, the gate of gifts had been closed
behind him. He is what he is, and nothing more. Yet wounds,
Emerson had said years before in his essay on "Compensation," can become weapons. People of all kinds rise to emi-
nence. Why? "You must elect your own work; you shall
take what your brain can, and drop all the rest," he would
advise in 1860 in "Power." Only then "can that amount of
vital force accumulate which can make the step from knowing to doing." But how is that step to be made? What raises
one person above another when all have immediate access to
indwelling truth? "No object interests us but man," Emerson
would say in his essay on "Beauty," and of "man only in his
superiorities." But how are superiorities to be identified?

That question engaged Emerson for much of his life. He
began to formulate a theory of human greatness in his boyhood, and he spoke of it often in his young manhood. In a
series of essays in 1835 on "Tests of Great Men," he celebrated people like Michelangelo, Luther, and Milton who
worked in concert with the universal spirit. He considered
the subject often again, most forcefully perhaps in "The
American Scholar" and "Self-Reliance." During the years
between these writings and the publication of *Representative
Men* in 1850 he pondered over the problem again and again
in his journals, rephrasing old certainties, that the complete

person is one who best achieves confident self-reliance, which is God-reliance. He knew that people may be equal in spirit but not in achievement. In his fifties he wondered in his essay on "Wealth" whether the "manly part" was but "to do with might and main what you can." An indisputable observation, perhaps, but not quite the answer to the question.

On the subject of human greatness, as on all others, Emerson speaks often as a person who has had revelation of truth, and only seeks the proper words to communicate it. He circles back to old assumptions, moving beyond them, and then circles back again with some new assurance, moving in a spiral upward toward clearer expression of what he knows to be true. His first and last concern was with the nature of the superior person, the person who stood as representative not of what all people could be, the gate of gifts having been closed behind them at birth, but of that toward which they might aspire and through grace of circumstance perhaps attain.

The problem was important to Emerson because it embodied both his certainty of possibilities for excellence in the single, separate person and his distrust of the mass. The person, not the mass, attains superiority. The mass follows. Emerson's concern about the secret of human greatness has been described as both a declaration of optimism and a cry for reassurance. It was his defense against himself, his share in every person's inevitable failure to become what he might, if he had been stronger or healthier, less dissipated or less bound by duty to others. It was an expression of all people's ancient adulation of heroes who could do what they could not do and of their hungry admiration or envy of wisdom or courage or success beyond their own, of a Prometheus, a redeemer, a person somehow larger in wisdom or strength whom they might follow with confident assurance.

"Nature seems to exist only for the excellent," said Emerson in explaining "The Uses of Great Men" in the

Ralph Waldo Emerson

introductory chapter of *Representative Men.* "The world is upheld by the veracity of good men: they make the earth wholesome. . . . Life is sweet and tolerable only in our belief in such society; and, actually or ideally, we manage to live with superiors," who "inhabit a higher sphere of thought, into which other men rise with labor and difficulty." Each great person is "what he is from nature." He "never reminds us of others." He is "constructive, fertile, magnetic." But in all of human history had there ever been an unmistakably great man? There had been "meditative men of an intuitive manner of thought." There had been men who knew that self-reliance was God-reliance. Not overwhelmed by the influence of power "to dazzle and blind the beholder," they had offered new entries to freedom to their contemporaries. But once gone, could they be replaced?

Each generation must widen its horizon through the leadership of people who represent its unique concern with glory or rapaciousness. The great man would inevitably rise to new necessity. For greatness is implicit in all persons who, conscious of limitations, combine intelligence with insight. One generation's great man will not do for another generation: "With each new mind a new secret of nature transpires." Idolatry of great men can be dangerous, retrospective, warping a person's will to self-reliance, rendering him through imitation an intellectual suicide. "Every hero," said Emerson, "becomes a bore at last." Better name him as representative of his time and calling, instructive "first of things, and secondly, of ideas."

For several years in the United States and England Emerson had been delivering a series of lectures on great men of the past who had influenced their time, setting patterns which called for improvement. Collected in 1850 in *Representative Men,* they presented Plato as exemplar of the philosopher, Swedenborg as the mystic, Montaigne as the skeptic, Shakespeare as the poet, Napoleon as the man of the world, and Goethe as the writer.

With one exception, the order is chronological. Emerson

158

had been tempted to present Jesus as the mystic. Indeed, it has been suggested that, above all others, Jesus was Emerson's representative man. But he knew that the kind of presentation of Jesus that he in honesty would have to make would not be popularly received. He feared that knowledge of the inevitable antagonism of readers to what he would be impelled to say of Jesus, as man, would get in the way of his saying it truly. It would take "great gifts,—steadiest insight and perfect temper" to cut through the strong strands of theology and deification which bound Jesus to the hearts and minds of many of Emerson's audience. Consciousness of their want of sympathy might, he feared, make him "petulant or sore, in spite of himself," so he substituted Swedenborg instead, lamenting the theological bias that "fatally narrowed his interpretation of nature."

For each of Emerson's representative men was flawed. As much as any of the fictional characters or self-representations of Emerson's contemporaries of the 1850s each was ridden by some demon of limitation. None was whole; none rose to ultimate expectation; each was partial.

Plato, though a "balanced soul" who could see two answers to every question, out of whom "come all things that are still written and debated among men of thought," who recognize that "the fairest fortune that can befall man is to be guided by his daemon to that which is truly his own," is finally too literary, not prophetically authoritative. He had no system: "one man thinks he means this, and another that." In explaining Plato, Emerson has sometimes been suspected of explaining himself, who was described by one of his later contemporaries as a man without a handle. For Emerson, "Plato was philosophy, and philosophy Plato,—at once the glory and the shame of mankind." But whatever his faults, so much like Emerson's own, in failing to solve the enigma of existence, Plato was expansive: "He represents the privilege of the intellect, the power, namely, of carrying up every fact to successive platforms and so disclosing in every fact the germ of expansion." That is the very essence of thought, of progress, to build lasting ideological structures on the foundation of intuition.

Swedenborg—eccentric, saintly—had insights that he was unable to express. He saw nature as "wreathing through an everlasting spiral, with wheels that never dry, on axles that never creak." He recognized, as Emerson did, that "the physical world was purely symbolical of the spiritual world," but allowed himself to be trapped by assurance that his was a voice uniquely endowed to utter truths repetitively, so that at last he became retrospective, shuffling mournfully among the bones of his own dead prose, shackled by theologic determination. Montaigne, the skeptic, recognized life as a pitching of pennies, a game to be prudently played, and which he played well. Honest, open-eyed, he saw life as it was, soiled by pride and ambition, and he wrote of what he saw with sincere simplicity. Of Montaigne's *Essais*, Emerson said, "I know not anywhere a book that seems less written. It is the language of conversation transferred to a book." Though not a man who put great faith in matters of spirit, Montaigne knew that "through evil agents, through toys and atoms, a great and beneficent tendency irresistibly springs."

To the younger Emerson, Plato and platonism had seemed to point attractively toward truth; now older he turned with special pleasure to Montaigne, the practical, plain-spoken man, incapable of mesmeric deception, who so well set forth the other, more worldly portion of truth. Unlike Shakespeare's, his was not a waste of talent. Shakespeare, who "wrote airs for all our modern music" and "the text of modern life," a man of insight and great ability, capable of finding truth in beauty, "converted the elements which waited on his command into entertainments," to become "master of the revels of mankind, . . . using his genius for public amusement." Like Swedenborg's his was a half-view: "The world still waits its poet-priest, a reconciler, who shall not trifle with Shakespeare the player, nor grope in graves with Swedenborg; but shall see, speak, and act, with equal inspiration."

Napoleon, completely modern, endowed with great gifts of power, turned that power to evil ends. The world was finally no better for his having lived in it. Lacking moral principles, he inevitably failed, as "every experiment . . . that has a sensual and selfish end will fail." Napoleon's had been a heaving, struggling, merciless, self-aggrandizing kind of middle life, grim, dark, deceitful, and perilous, but played out with wondrous excitement and devious skill. The corrupted epitome of man reaching for power, he not only represented his time, but anticipated the power barons who were beginning to arise in the New World. "We are always in trouble," explained Emerson, "always in a bad plight, just on the brink of destruction and only to be saved by invention and courage." These Napoleon had in plenty, but his overreaching misuse of self-confidence finally led to his downfall. Potentially great, meeting the challenge of his time, his end was humiliation and disgrace.

Napoleon's contemporary Goethe was not a man of power, except in words. His gift allowed him to be the "secretary of mankind, who is to report the doings of the wonderful spirit of life that everywhere throbs and works." As reporter, he was not participant, only observer, often a "sycophant ducking to the giddy opinion of a restless people." Goethe, thought Emerson, had great skill with words, and "said the best things about nature that ever were said." Much of his poetry was superb. Much of his prose was of "delicious sweetness." Few exceeded him in talent, but, said Emerson, "Talent alone cannot make a writer. There must be a man behind the book; a personality which by birth and quality is pledged to the doctrine there set forth." Goethe had not "worshipped at the highest unity"; was "incapable of self-surrender to the moral sentiment." Like Napoleon, he was entirely at home in his century, a stern

Ralph Waldo Emerson

realist, a man of his time to whom his time responded. He had courage to report and skill at adaptation. He was artistic but not an artist. "I count him a great man," said Emerson, "who inhabits a higher sphere of thought, into which other men rise with labor and difficulty."

But he found none "in all the procession of famous men," completely to provide "reason or illumination, or that essence we were looking for." The great man was he in whom other people discovered potentialities within themselves that they had not before known. What Emerson discovered were only representative men, equipped to grasp at opportunities provided by their place, their moment. The moment inevitably retrogressing and new moments progressively taking its place, each required fresh revelation. Today is today, and feeds warily on its yesterdays: "great men exist that there may be greater men."

Late in life, twenty years after *Representative Men,* Emerson delivered at Harvard in 1870 his lectures on "The Natural History of the Intellect," which approached again the subject of human greatness. "In unfit company," he says, "the finest powers are paralyzed. No ambition, no opposition, no friendly attention and fostering kindness, no wine, music, or exhilarating aids, neither warm fireside nor fresh air, walking or riding, avail at all to resist the palsy of mis-association." When the circumstance does not call the man, "genius is dull; there is no genius. . . . Wisdom is like electricity." He conceded finally that "there is no permanent wise man, but men capable of wisdom, who being put into certain company or other favorable conditions becomes wise, as glasses rubbed acquire power for a time."

Bound by necessity, a person serves by waiting. But circumstance does not completely bind. People are ordained by fate to be free when each recognizes mind as the creator of the world, and when prudence or circumstance supplies health and leisure which allow recognition of the harmonious relation of all things revealed through hushed attendance to the voice of the God within. For the mind, Emerson reminded his audience, is continuously creating: "Each man is a new power in Nature. He holds the keys of the world in his hands. No quality in Nature's vast magazines he cannot touch, no truth he cannot see. Silent, impassive, even sulkily Nature offers her gift to man. She is immensely rich; he is welcome to her entire goods, but she speaks no word, will not so much as beckon or cough; only this, she is careful to leave the door ajar. . . . If he takes her hint and uses her goods she speaks no word; if he blunders and starves she says nothing. To the idle blockhead Nature is poor, sterile, inhospitable. To the gardener her loam is all strawberries, pears, pineapples. To the miller her rivers whirl the wheel and weave carpets and broadcloth. To the sculptor her stones are soft. . . . To the poet all sounds and words are melodies and rhythms. In her hundred gated Thebes every chamber is a new door."

Entering the world, with the gate of gifts closed at birth, each person owns a single key, useless to any but himself, but it can open doors which lead toward vistas undiscovered before: "Herein is the wealth of each," explained Emerson. "His equipment, though new, is complete; his prudence his own; his courage, his charity are his own. He has his own defenses and his own fangs; his perception and his own mode of reply to sophistries. Whilst he draws on his own he cannot be overshadowed or supplanted." Imitation, Emerson had said many years earlier, is suicide. "Echo the leaders," he adds now, "and they will fast enough see that you have nothing for them. . . . The one thing not to be forgiven to intellectual persons is that they believe the ideas of others. . . . Profound sincerity is the only basis of talent as of character."

This was not new, only a restatement of what Emerson had been circling toward for almost forty years. How remarkably consistent he continued to remain. He had early spoken of a "foolish consistency" as the "hobgoblin of little minds." His own consistency was a circling outward, discovering new conclusions from old premises. He had from the beginning known that the self-reliant man would stand on his own feet, think his own thoughts, never imitate. But to what purpose?

Most simply put, the answer to that question is that every person must prepare himself by recognition and exercise of whatever talent he possesses so that when that talent is needed, he can step forward to become for the moment the necessary person. Many must be prepared, though few chosen. The great person is the self-reliant, concentrative person who is able to rise to leadership when his unique talents respond to temporal requirements. He is representative because he knows that what is then true for him in his own heart responds to what is necessary to his place, his time, his moment.

He need not be a perfect man. Indeed, he is inevitably partial, but he recognizes and acts upon that within himself that is uniquely his. Perhaps it is only power, such as Napoleon had. But the person is not the quality, only its agent. Napoleon represented power, but he was not power. "We love," explained Emerson, "but we are not love. . . . Goethe, the unsurpassing intellect of modern times, apprehends the spiritual but is not spiritual." Each to his own, and balance is then inevitable. Properly self-reliant people represent a storehouse from which necessity can draw at will. Nature rejects what does not fit her scheme, or accepts it temporarily until equilibrium can be reached, and then she throws it aside as she threw Bonaparte aside. Each man's gift which he lays at the altar of the world is received or neglected according to the world's need. If it is the dross of imitation, it is worthless; if it is his own, it is there, ready for use when and if the world calls for it.

Man's duty, then, to himself and to the world, is preparation, the making the best of what gifts he has been allowed. "There are two theories of life," Emerson explains, "one for the demonstration of our talent, the other for the education of men. One is activity, the busy-body, the following of that practical talent which we have, in the belief that what is so natural, easy and pleasant to us and desirable to others will surely lead us out safely; in this direction is usefulness, comfort, society, low power of all sorts. The other is trust, religion, consent to be nothing for eternity, entranced waiting, and worship of ideas. This is solitary, grand, secular. They are in perpetual balance and strife." Emerson had said much the same thing more succinctly ten years before in his essay on "Wealth," where he explained that the "manly part is to do with might and main what you can do."

The great man, then, is he who through reliance on the best within him prepares himself for the contributions which he can uniquely make toward the better realization of whatever in his time is revealed as truth. He will walk humbly and obey his God, the God within. Because he is a man of his time, molded by the limitations of his time, he may speak as a representative of that time when, and only when, the particular gift which he has to offer fits the necessity of the time, and when he is prepared to listen to the spirit within, to receive revelation, however brief, of truths which do pass present understanding but which he recognizes as truth which properly translated is eternal.

If he speaks to his time so that others respond to him, so much the better for his time, and he is recognized and remembered as having pointed toward possibilities of human excellence. He may not be correct. His voice may falter or his talents fail. But he is prepared to answer the call of his contemporaries. If not called, the potentiality for greatness nevertheless exists. His compensation is that he has lived and thought and acted according to the best of his capacity. For whatever other reason had he been born?

Emerson in 1870 was somewhat more somber when he then advised that the "first rule is to obey your genius," than he had been almost thirty years earlier when he had challenged, "Insist on yourself; never imitate. . . . Nothing can bring you peace but yourself. Nothing can bring you peace but the triumph of principles." The country in which Emerson had lived and suffered and spoken during those years had struggled through wars, rapacity, and cupidity, and Emerson had walked quietly along with it, recognizing its inevitable ailments, but his recommendations for cure remaining unchanged.

In one of his last addresses, in 1878, he announced, "What this country longs for is personalities, grand persons to counteract its materialities. . . . 'Tis not free institutions, 'tis not democracy that is the end—no, but only the means." What is wanted are persons "of original perception and original action," for the "flowering of civilization is the finished man."

The words are different, but the compelling voice remains the same: "I have little esteem for governments. . . . I put the private man first." His faith never faltered in the infinite possibilities of the single, separate person. Cure him, cure all. He never abandoned assurance that what was insightfully true for each was inevitably true for all, because there is one supernal inward flowing mind available to every person.

These premises have weathered many tempting trials at rebuttal. But Emerson stands confidently, his feet firmly planted, challenging our retrospective age to find him wrong. There is little nourishment in gnawing on the bones of our ancestors. Emerson is not of our time, but his voice still speaks as a reminder of the crippling disadvantages of fate and of possibilities for surmounting them. To honor Emerson, we move beyond him, remembering him as the center from which, each in our eccentric way, we have circled. He opened gates that have not yet been closed. His invitation remains, to recognize oneself as oneself. That is fulfillment.

The mark of greatness is an ability to respond to the requirements of one's time. On this Emerson insists, leaving a legacy, presenting a challenge. He invites others to move

The Mark of Greatness

beyond him, and others have. But to understand American thought, its vagaries, its repetitious circlings, its vaunting self-assurance and its search for tradition, its skills at advancement and retreat, an understanding of Emerson is important, for his voice most clearly articulates both sides of an argument that continues to engage his countrymen.

He spoke of facts and appearances, of possibilities for freedom and of fetters of fate, of life as it might be lived and of life as it is shamelessly squandered, of what people may do to nature and what nature can do to people. He moves back and forth between two poles, luring toward one with siren words, but warning also of jagged rocks against which self-fascinated people can be battered. Emerson is one of those artists of whom Lionel Trilling speaks, who maintain a dialectic within themselves, "their meaning and power lying in their contradictions," so that "they contain within themselves . . . the very essence of the culture which has produced them, "and the sign of this," says Trilling, "is that they do not serve the ends of any one ideological group or tendency." This is not to say that they are all things to all men, but that they illuminate and intensify and discover fresh applications for relationships between spirit and reality which are so complex as to be ultimately inexplicable, except in terms of art. It is dialogue of this kind that constitutes a culture or a civilization, in this instance what is customarily called American or, more properly, Western civilization.

Emerson was an artist, not a thinker. His ideas were probably the least important thing about him, for they were shared, to one degree or another, with many others of his time, with Melville and Poe and Bronson Alcott, with Coleridge, Carlyle, and Goethe. Sometimes one or another of these others presented part of the dialogue better than Emerson did, but few presented it more completely or with more fluid grace or continuing charm. In sincerity, he spoke what he perceived, sometimes this, at other times that, so that Walt Whitman could learn from Emerson to say, "Do

Ralph Waldo Emerson

I contradict myself? Very well, I contradict myself." What else can a person do, if he is to be honest?

Despite his high regard for intelligence, for man thinking, for the tremendous revolutionary power of idea, Emerson finally distrusts thought. The best any man, even Plato, can do is to discover that all things are alike and all things different, and to explain, through honest reporting of honest perceptions, just how they resemble one another, yet how each is unique; to discover that a world striving toward unity is characterized by variety, that existence is fragmented by intellect, that fate is opposed to freedom, that genius is single but talent multiple, that God is one but man's notions of him various, so that every person must see two sides to every object, two directions to every thought, attempting a practical synthesis, but knowing that the bridge he builds will not bear the final weight of truth. For thinking makes a fool of a man when he supposes his thought to be more than opinion, a shadowed image of reality.

For this reason scientists and poets are more likely than the rest of us to recognize the usefulness of Emerson's dialectic, for however blunt his tools, he worked with many of the same materials that they use. Those of us who would remake the world to our own partial image of what it should be may very well discover him an embarrassment and an encumbrance—this man Emerson, who shares our vision of what man might be, but who also knows that this bad and badly managed world is man's burden and delight, and that its evils can only be avoided when we shut our eyes to them.

Suggestions for Further Reading

IF I WERE TO BEGIN reading Emerson, I think that I would start with his "The American Scholar," certainly among the hardiest and most influential of his essays. From there I would go to his collection of *Essays* of 1841, reading that volume not as a miscellany, but as a book complete, each essay leading toward the next, and the last circling back to the first. Then I think that I would read his essay on "The Poet" in *Essays, Second Series,* and the essay on "Experience" in the same volume, following these with the essays on "Fate" and "Illusion" that introduce and conclude *The Conduct of Life.* These will supply foundations on which each reader can build, some puzzling over Emerson's poetry, others exploring further through his prose, to argue or admire. If any discovers in him exactly the same person that I have discovered, I shall be greatly surprised.

The most pleasant biography of Emerson is his friend Oliver Wendell Holmes's *Ralph Waldo Emerson* (Boston and New York: Houghton Mifflin and Company, 1885). The most meticulously correct is Ralph Leslie Rusk's *The Life of Ralph Waldo Emerson* (New York: Columbia University Press, 1949). The most critically provocative is Stephen E. Whicher's *Freedom and Fate: An Inner Life of Ralph Waldo Emerson* (Philadelphia: University of Pennsylvania Press, 1953).

Other books that may be found useful are

ANDERSON, JOHN Q. *The Liberating Gods: Emerson on Poets and Poetry*. Coral Gables: University of Miami Press, 1971.

BROOKS, VAN WYCK. *The Life of Emerson.* New York: E. P. Dutton & Co., 1932.

CHAPMAN, JOHN JAY. *Emerson and Other Essays.* New York: Charles Scribners' Sons, 1898; reprint, New York: AMS Press, 1965.

Ralph Waldo Emerson

DERLETH, AUGUST WILLIAM. *Emerson, Our Contemporary.* New York: Crowell-Collier Press, 1970.

DUNCAN, JEFFREY L. *The Power and Form of Emerson's Thought.* Princeton, N.J.: Princeton University Press, 1973.

GAY, ROBERT M. *Emerson: A Study of the Poet as Seer.* New York: Doubleday, Doran and Company, 1928.

HOPKINS, VIVIAN C. *Spires of Form: Emerson's Aesthetic Theory.* Cambridge, Mass.: Harvard University Press, 1951.

MATTHIESSEN, F. O. *American Renaissance: Art and Expression in the Age of Emerson and Whitman.* London, Toronto, New York: Oxford University Press, 1941.

MILES, JOSEPHINE. *Ralph Waldo Emerson.* Minneapolis: University of Minnesota Press, 1964.

PAUL, SHERMAN. *Emerson's Angle of Vision: Man and Nature in American Experience.* Cambridge, Mass.: Harvard University Press, 1952.

PORTE, JOEL. *Ralph Waldo Emerson and His Time.* New York: Oxford University Press, 1978.

PORTER, DAVID. *Emerson and Literary Change.* Cambridge, Mass.: Harvard University Press, 1978.

SCHEICK, WILLIAM J. *The Slender Human Words: Emerson's Artistry in Prose.* Knoxville: University of Tennessee Press, 1978.

WAGENKNECHT, EDWARD C. *Ralph Waldo Emerson: Portrait of a Balanced Soul.* New York: Oxford University Press, 1974.

WAGGONER, HYATT HOWE. *Emerson as Poet.* Princeton, N.J.: Princeton University Press, 1974.

YODER, R. A. *Emerson and the Orphic Poet in America.* Berkeley and Los Angeles: University of California Press, 1978.